WORD by WORD PRIMARY

PHONICS PICTURE DICTIONARY

Steven J. Molinsky • Bill Bliss

Illustrated by
Richard E. Hill
Maya Shorr Katz

Longman

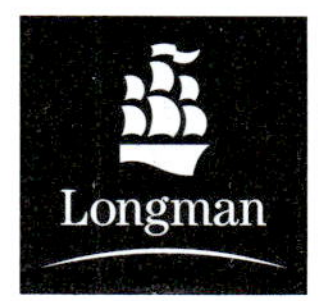

INTRODUCTION

The *Word by Word Primary Phonics Picture Dictionary* program offers a systematic, phonics-based curriculum presenting over 1000 words through lively and motivating illustrations. The program provides a comprehensive introduction to sound/letter association, phonograms (word families), decoding and word recognition, and vocabulary concepts and skills. While the program is designed for effective use by all children, its picture-based instruction and careful curriculum sequence are particularly appropriate for English language learners and other special needs students studying in school, small-group, tutorial, and family learning settings.

The program consists of the Phonics Picture Dictionary, Workbooks at three levels, an Audio Program, Phonics Picture/Word Cards, a Song Album, a Tutor's Handbook, and a Teacher's Guide that includes chants, rhymes, and reproducible activity masters and tests. These materials are designed to serve as a teacher's main resource for short, explicit phonics-based lessons (perhaps 10-15 minutes) as an adjunct to other ongoing reading and language instruction.

TEACHING STRATEGIES

The core learning device in the dictionary is a lesson consisting of words and pictures accompanied by an illustrated phrase or sentence at the bottom of the page. Specific teaching strategies vary for each lesson and are covered in the Teacher's Guide. Some general suggestions are:

Introduce the Lesson: Tell children the lesson objective using simple language (such as "word families") rather than technical terms (such as "phonograms").

Present the Words: (For Unit 2, first use the appropriate Picture/Word Cards to build phonemic awareness through aural/oral practice in *segmenting* and *blending* sounds. Point to a picture, say each sound of the word separately, and have children repeat and practice. Then model how the sounds blend to make the word and have children repeat and practice.) For all units, say each word as children look at the word and picture in the dictionary and then have children repeat the word chorally and individually. Say the word again slowly and have children practice *tracking* aurally by pointing to each letter as its sound is heard. Then have children practice blending as they read each word aloud.

Discuss Word Meanings and Pictures: For each word, have children describe what they see in the picture. Talk about the context and extend vocabulary as appropriate. Ask questions such as, "What color is the fruit?" or "Why do you think he's angry?"

Analyze and Practice Word Structures: Say each word and have children count and identify the separate sounds (and later, syllables) that make up the word. On the board, write the word with extra space or a plus sign between each letter or combination of letters that represents a separate sound. Have children practice *tracking* by pointing to the letter(s) that represent a sound as you say each word slowly. Have them practice *blending* by saying the words aloud, smoothly combining the separate sounds to form each word.

Make Sentences: Have children think of sentences for each word and share them orally (not in writing).

Spelling Partners: Have children work in pairs to check each other's ability to spell the words in the lesson.

The Illustrated Phrase or Sentence: Have children look at the illustration and talk about the characters, setting, and situation. Read the phrase or sentence slowly and have children practice *tracking* each separate word. Then have children practice reading aloud. Have fun with the illustrations and use them for discussions, role-play skits, and prompts for original student artwork or writing.

Spelling & Dictation Quiz: Use the words for spelling homework and quizzes based on these predictable letter-sound associations.

Chants & Rhymes: The lesson's chant or rhyme appears in the Teacher's Guide and on the Audio Program. Have children listen and then practice chorally and individually.

Supplementary Practice: The Workbooks provide activities for writing, listening, and reading decodable text. The Audio Program and Song Album provide valuable listening, reading, chanting, and singing practice. The Teacher's Guide offers expansion activities, games, reproducible activity masters, and assessment tools.

We hope that the *Word by Word Primary Phonics Picture Dictionary* program helps you create for your students a phonics-based learning experience that is effective, interactive, responsive to students' different strengths and learning styles . . . and fun!

Steven J. Molinsky
Bill Bliss

Library of Congress Cataloging-in-Publication Data
Molinsky, Steven J.
Word by word primary phonics picture dictionary / Steven J. Molinsky, Bill Bliss ; illustrated by Richard E. Hill, Maya Shorr Katz.
p. cm.
Summary: A phonics-based presentation of over 1000 English words through illustrations, including an introduction to phonemic awareness, decoding and word recognition,and vocabulary concepts and skills development.
ISBN 0-13-022206-2. -- ISBN 0-13-022171-6 (pbk.)
1. Picture dictionaries, English Juvenile literature.
[1. Picture dictionaries.] I. Bliss, Bill. II. Hill,Richard E., PE1629.M584 2000
423'.1--dc21 99-15215
CIP

Editorial Director: *Louise Jennewine*
Executive Editor: *Anne Stribling*
Director of Design and Production: *Rhea Banker*
Associate Director of Electronic Publishing: *Aliza Greenblatt*
Production/Editorial Design Manager: *Paul Belfanti*
Production Manager: *Ray Keating*
Senior Manufacturing Manager: *Patrice Fraccio*
Manufacturing Buyer: *Dave Dickey*
Electronic Production Editors, Page Compositors, Interior Designers: *Paula Williams, Wendy Wolf*
Cover Designer: *Merle Krumper*
Cover Artists: *Richard E. Hill, Maya Shorr Katz, Carey Davies*
Scanners, Color Correctors: *Todd D. Ware, Robert W. Handago*
Production Assistant: *Robert Siek*
Manuscript Preparation Assistant: *Rose Ann Merrey*
Illustrations: *Richard E. Hill, Maya Shorr Katz*

Pearson Education, 10 Bank St., White Plains, NY 10606

Paperback ISBN 0-13-022171-6
Hardback ISBN 0-13-022206-2

Printed in the United States of America

10 9 8 7 6

Note:
Kindergarten-level lessons are in Units 1 & 2 and on pages 74, 80, 180–185.

UNIT 1

ALPHABET
&
CONCEPTS ABOUT PRINT

Alphabet

Uppercase Print
Lowercase Print
Uppercase Type
Lowercase Type

Concepts About Print

Top, Bottom, Left, Right
Letter, Word, Sentence, Page

A B C D E

F G H I J

K L M N O

P Q R S T

U V W X Y Z

a b c d e

f g h i j

k l m n o

p q r s t

u v w x y z

A B C D E

F G H I J

K L M N O

P Q R S T

U V W X Y Z

a b c d e

f g h i j

k l m n o

p q r s t

u v w x y z

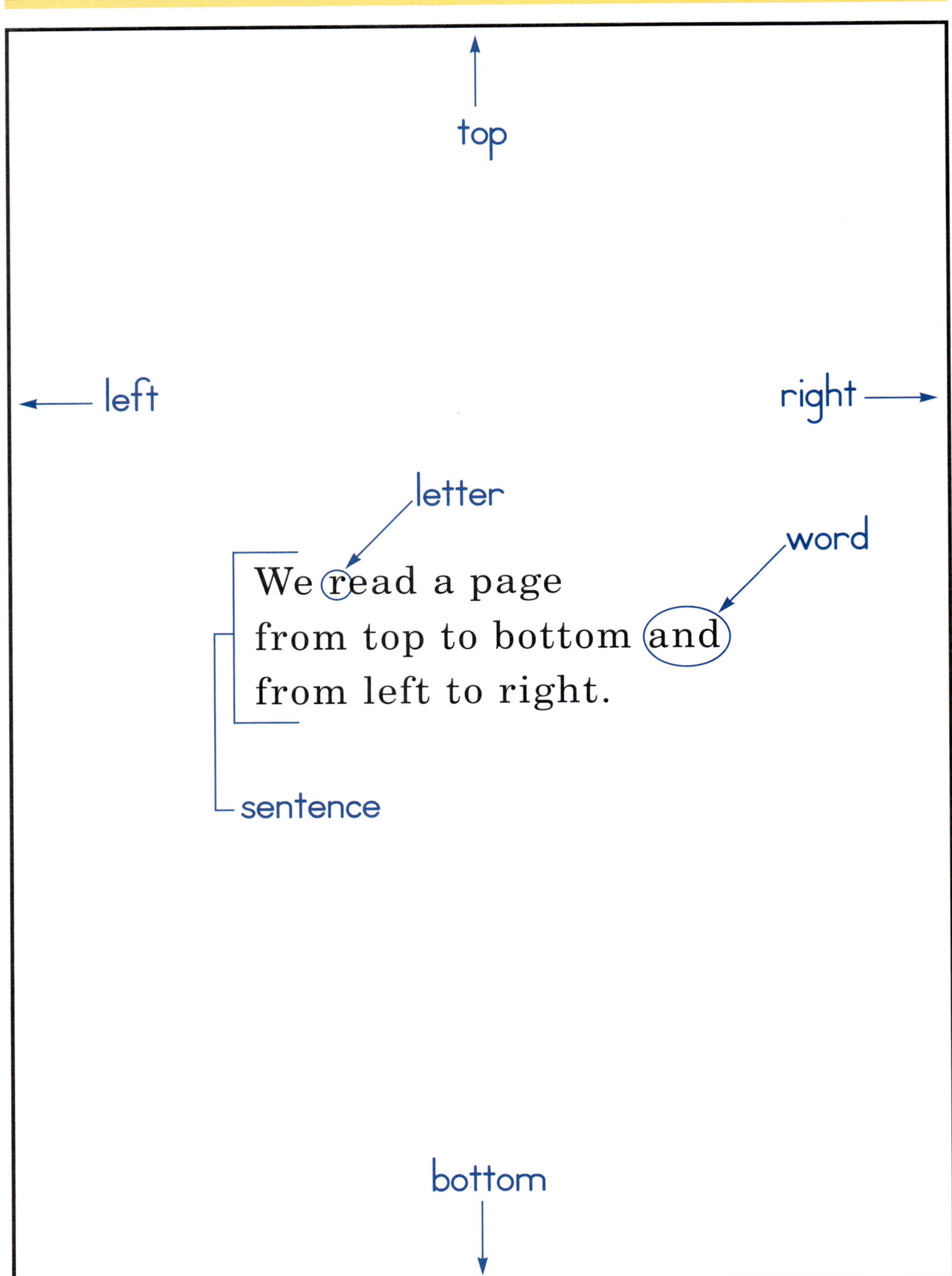
top
left
right
letter
word
We read a page
from top to bottom and
from left to right.
sentence
bottom

UNIT 2

SOUND/LETTER ASSOCIATION & PHONOGRAMS

Initial Consonants & Short Vowel Word Families

m, v + an
c, p + an
m, c, b + at
m, c, l + ap
p, b, w + ig
p, s, k + it
d, r, z + ip
p, w, f + in
l, f, h + og
c, p, h + ot
m, h, t + en
p, n, g + et
b, r, s + un
m, b, j, + ug

Short Vowel Word Families (Mixed Initial Consonants)

an
ap
at
ad
ag, am
ig
ip
it
ot
og, op
et
en
ug
un, ut
ub, up, ud

Initial Short Vowels

a, e, i, o, u

Blending Initial Consonants, Mixed Short Vowels, & Mixed Final Consonants

m + Short Vowel + Consonant
n + Short Vowel + Consonant
f + Short Vowel + Consonant
s + Short Vowel + Consonant
h + Short Vowel + Consonant
j + Short Vowel + Consonant
r + Short Vowel + Consonant
l + Short Vowel + Consonant
b + Short Vowel + Consonant
p + Short Vowel + Consonant
d + Short Vowel + Consonant
t + Short Vowel + Consonant
g + Short Vowel + Consonant
c, k + Short Vowel + Consonant

Review & Expansion

Consonants and Short Vowels: Review Chart with Pictures
Consonants and Short Vowels: Review Chart with Words
Rhyming Words
Changes in Words: Vowel Substitutions
Changes in Words: Consonant Substitutions
Changes in Words: Consonant & Vowel Substitutions

an

man

van

man van

a man in a van

an

c + a + n

can

pan

can pan

a can and a pan

at

m+a+t  mat

c+a+t  cat

b+a+t  bat

mat cat bat

a cat and a bat

m + a + p  map

c + a + p  cap

l + a + p 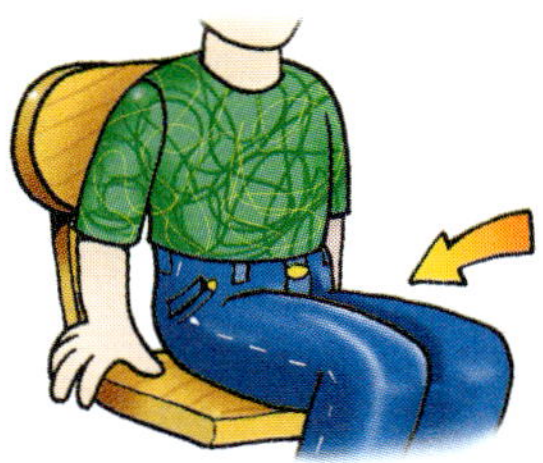 lap

map cap lap

a cap on a lap

ig

p + i + g  pig

b + i + g  big

w + i + g  wig

pig big wig

a big pig in a wig

p + i + t  pit

s + i + t  sit

k + i + t 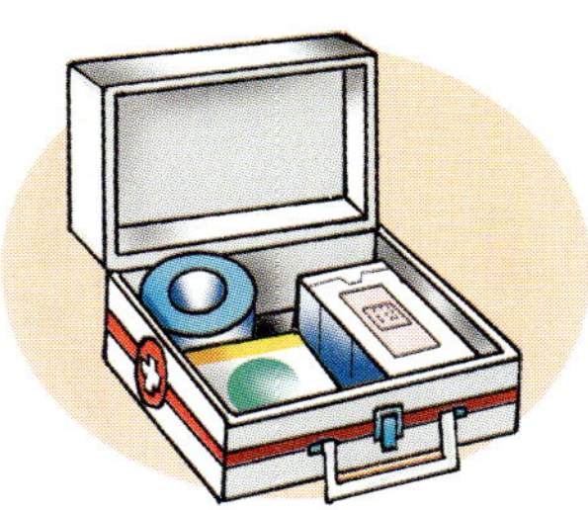 kit

pit sit kit

sit on a pit

d+i+p  dip

r+i+p  rip

z+i+p 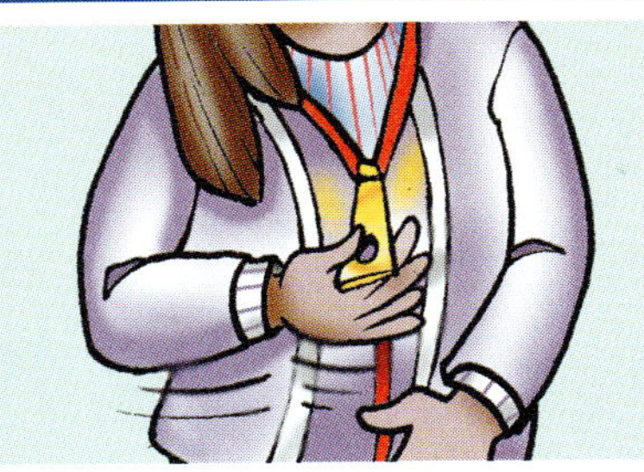 zip

dip rip zip

zip and rip

p+i+n  pin

w+i+n  win

 fin

pin win fin

a pin with a fin

og

l+o+g  log

f+o+g  fog

h+o+g  hog

log fog hog

a hog in the fog

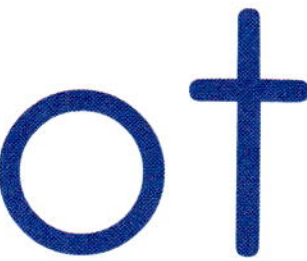

c+o+t 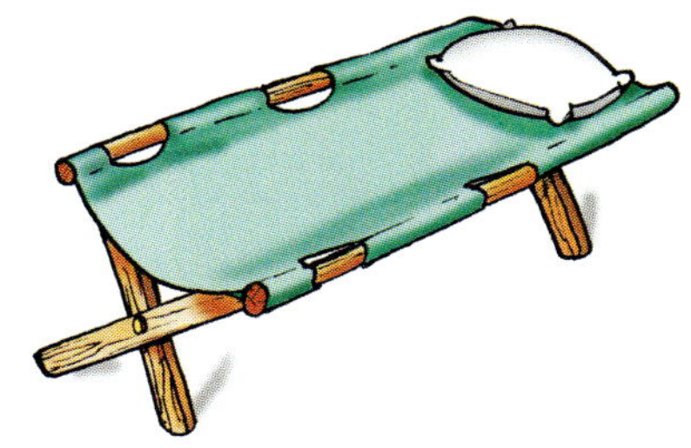 cot

p+o+t  pot

h+o+t  hot

cot pot hot

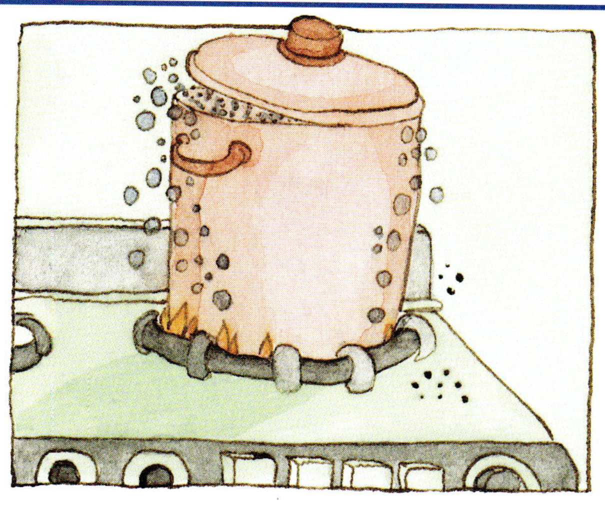

a hot pot

en

m + e + n  men

h + e + n  hen

t + e + n  ten

men hen ten

ten men and a hen

et

p + e + t  pet

n + e + t  net

g + e + t  get

pet net get

get a pet

un

b+u+n  bun

r+u+n  run

s+u+n  sun

bun run sun

run in the sun

ug

m+u+g  mug

b+u+g  bug

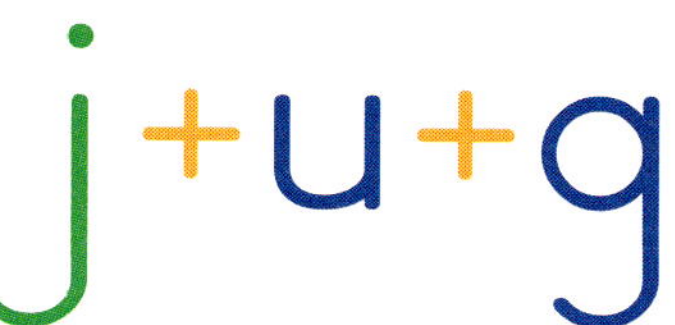

 jug

mug bug jug

a jug and a mug
and a bug

can

fan

man

pan

ran

← past tense

tan

van

can fan man pan ran tan van

Dan Jan Nan

 cap

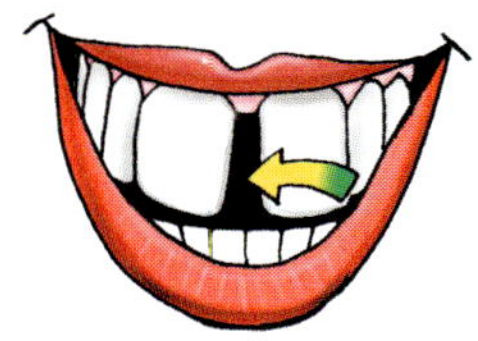 gap

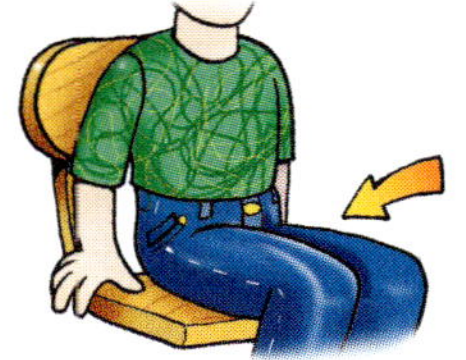 lap

 map

 nap

 rap

 sap

 tap

cap	gap	lap	map
nap	rap	sap	tap

 bat

 cat

 fat

 hat

 mat

 rat

 sat

 vat

bat cat fat hat mat rat sat vat

Nat Pat

ad

bad

dad

lad

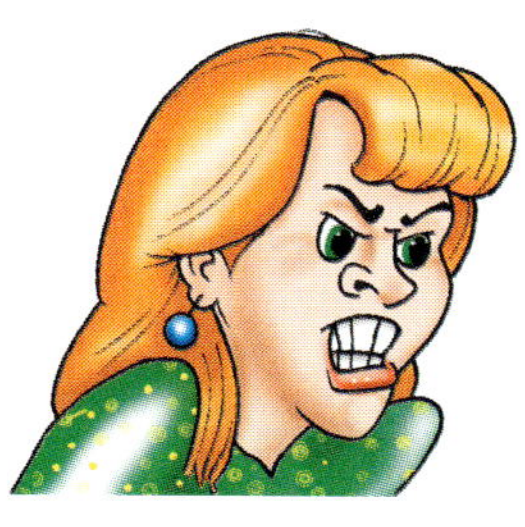

mad

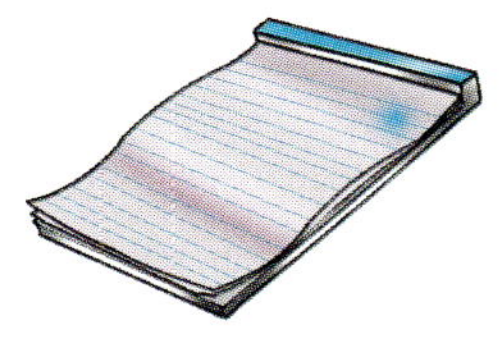

pad

sad

bad	dad	lad
mad	pad	sad

 bag

 rag

 tag

 wag

bag rag tag wag

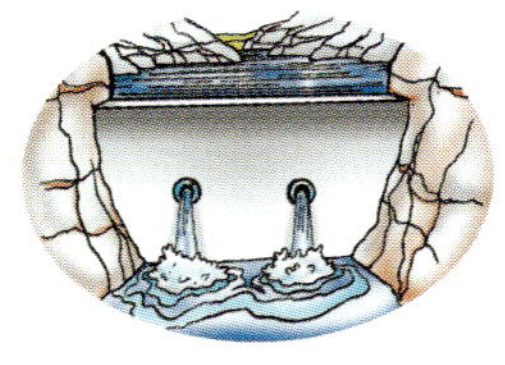 dam

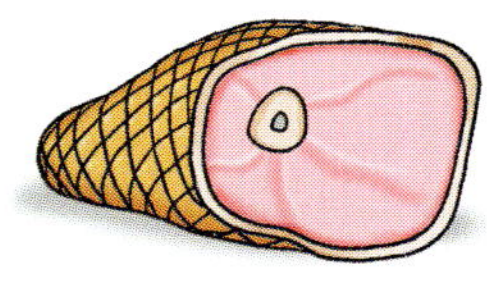 ham

 jam

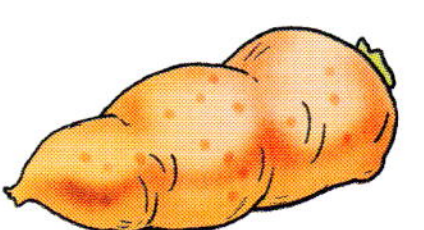 yam

dam ham jam yam Pam Sam

ig

big

dig

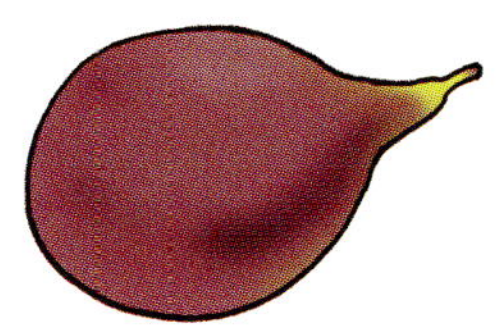

fig

jig

pig

rig

wig

big dig fig jig

pig rig wig

dip

hip

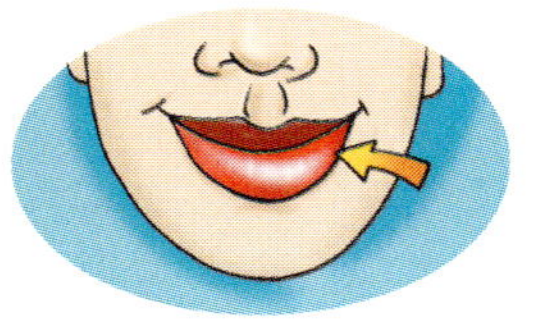

lip

rip

sip

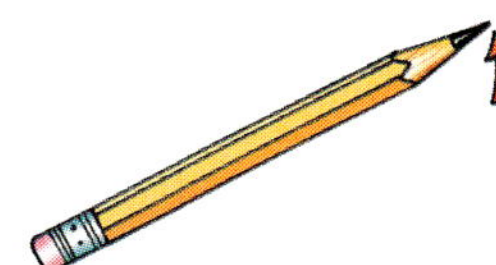

tip

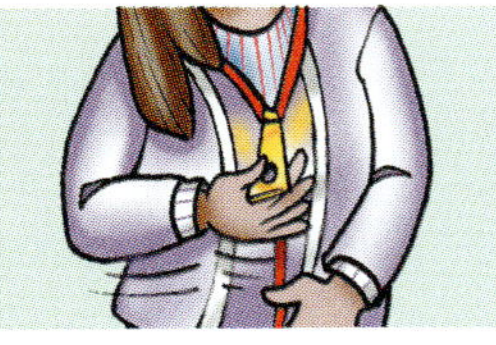

zip

dip hip lip rip

sip tip zip

 bit

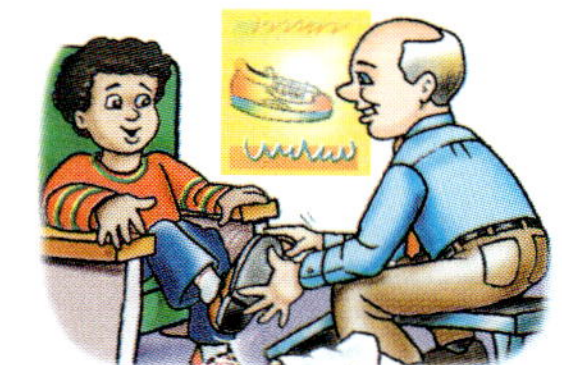 fit

 hit

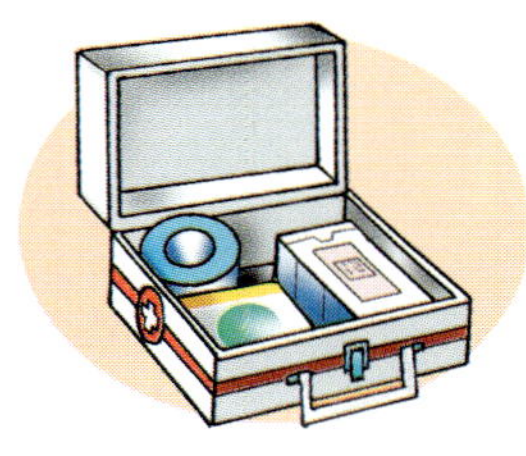 kit

 lit

 pit

 sit

 zit

bit	fit	hit	kit
lit	pit	sit	zit

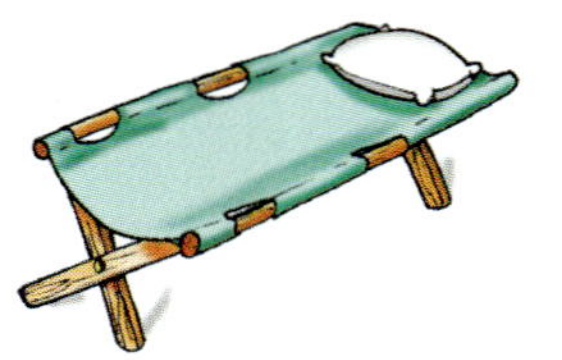

cot

dot

got

hot

lot

pot

tot

cot dot got hot

lot pot tot

og

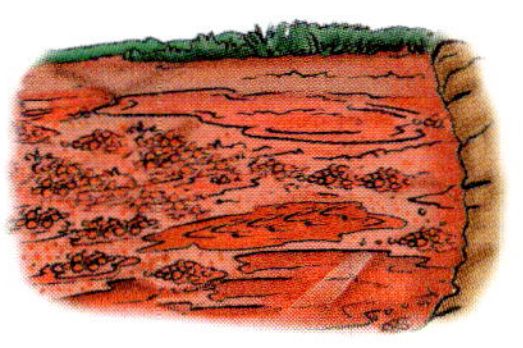 bog

 fog

 hog

 log

bog fog hog log

 hop

 mop

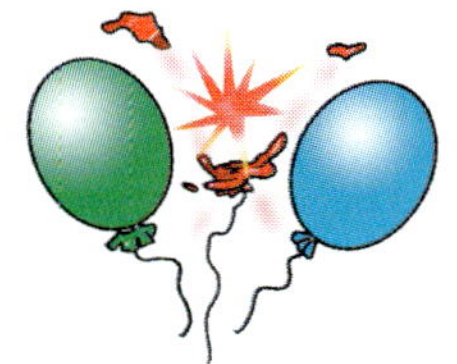 pop

 top

hop mop pop top

et

 get

 jet

 met

 net

 pet

 set

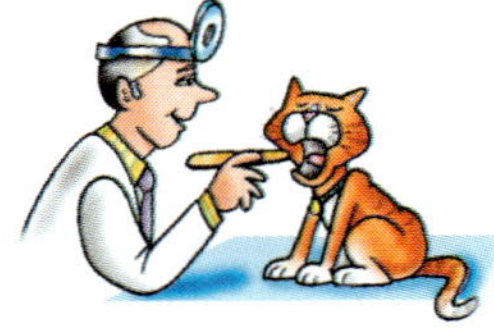 vet

 wet

get	jet	met	net
pet	set	vet	wet

en

den

hen

men

pen

ten

den hen men pen ten

Ben Ken Len

 bug

 dug

 hug

 jug

 mug

 rug

 tug

bug dug hug jug

mug rug tug

un

bun

fun

run

sun

bun fun run sun

ut

cut

hut

nut

rut

cut hut nut rut

 cub

 rub

 sub

 tub

cub rub sub tub

up ud

 cup

 pup

 bud

 mud

cup pup bud mud

add

ant

e

Ed

egg

i

ill

inch

o

odd

on

u

up

us

An ant is on an egg.

		man		mat
e		men		met
i		mill	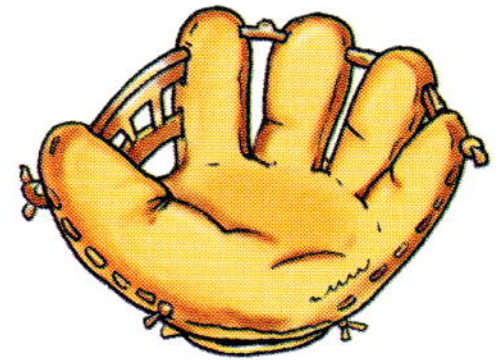	mitt
o		mom		mop
u		mud		mug

A man with a mop is in the mill.

 nap  Nat

e  net  neck

i  nit  Nick

o 

nod  not

u  nut

The nut is in the net.

a	fan		fat
e	fed		fell
i	fig		fin
o	fog		
u	fun		

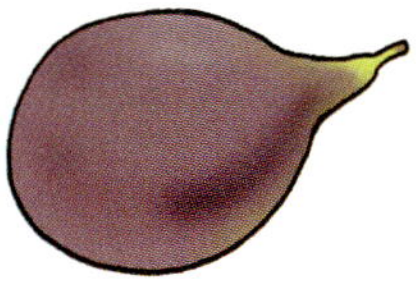

The fat fig fell.

a		sad		sat
e		set		sell
i		sip		sit
o		sob	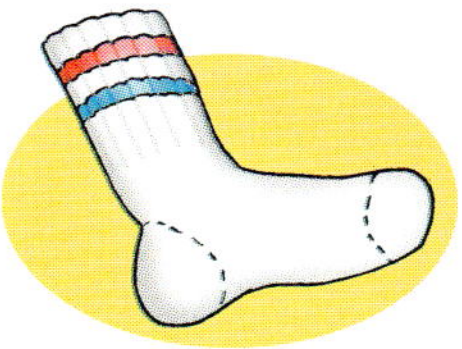	sock
u		sub		sun

The sad sock
sat in the sun.

a	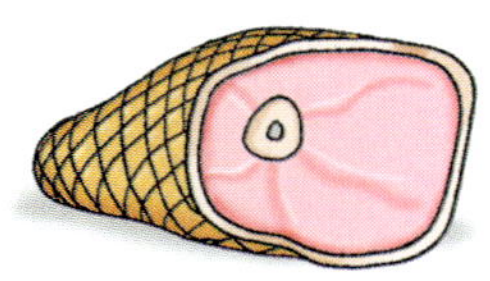	ham		hat
e		hem		hen
i		hip		hit
o		hog		hop
u		hug		hut

The hen hit the hog with a hat.

a		jam		Jack
e		jet		Jeff
i		jig		Jill
o		job		jog
u		jug		

Jill and Jeff jog.

a		ran		rat
e	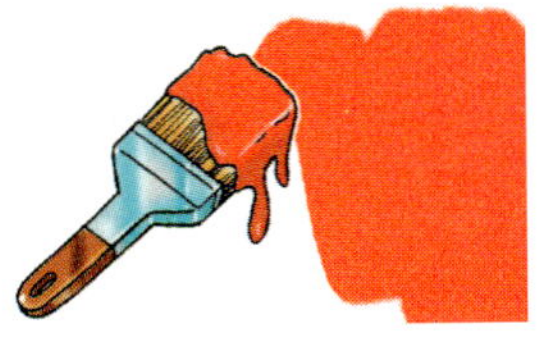	red		
i		rig		rip
o	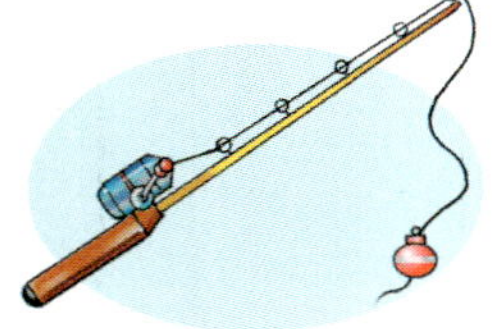	rod		rock
u		rug		run

The rat ran to the red rock.

a		lad	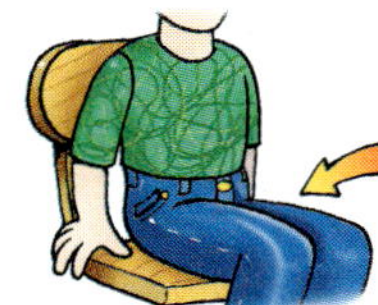	lap
e		led		leg
i	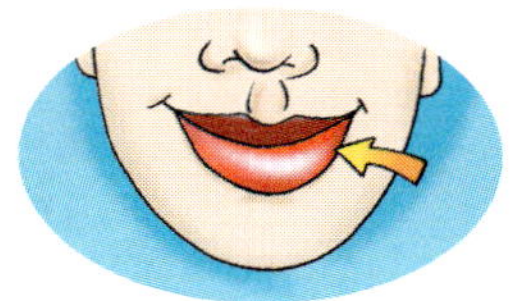	lip		lit
o		log		lot
u		luck		

The lad sat on the log in the lot.

a		bag		bat
e		bed		beg
i	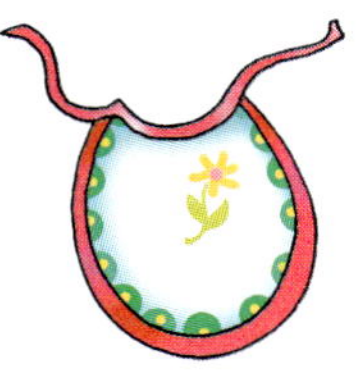	bib		big
o		Bob	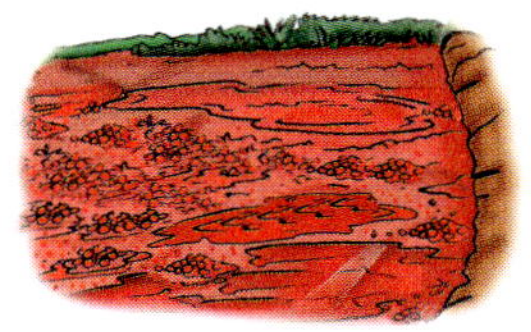	bog
u		bug		bus

A big bug is on the bed.

a	pad	pan
e	pen	pet
i	pig	pin
o	pop	pot
u	pup	

The pig and the pup
pop it with a pin.

a		dad	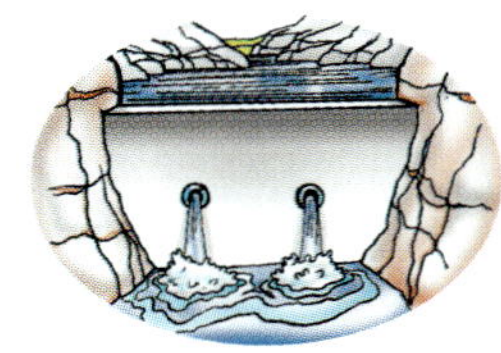	dam
e		den		
i		dig		dip
o		dot		doll
u		dug		duck

The duck and the pup dig and dig.

a		tag		tan
e		ten		tell
i	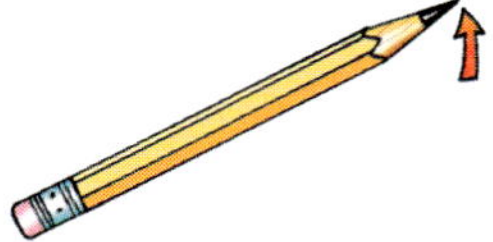	tip		tick
o		top		tot
u		tub		tug

The tot is in the tub with a top.

 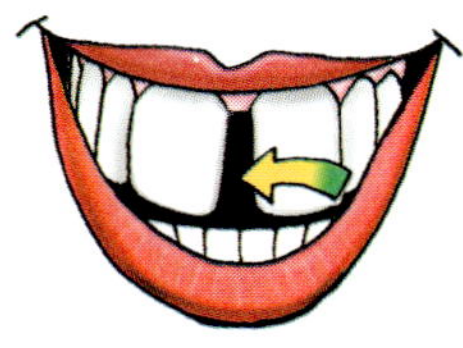 gap  gas

e  get

i  gill

o  got

u 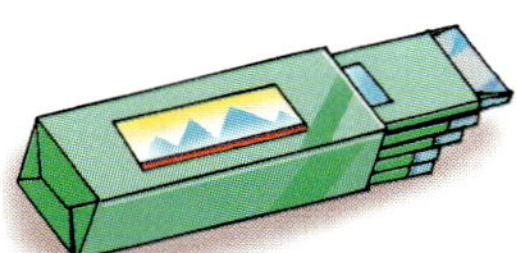 gum  gull

Get gas!

a	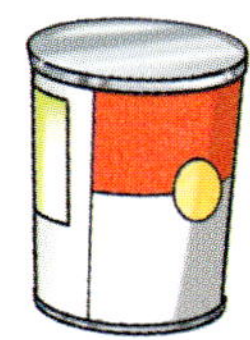	can		cat
e		Ken		
i		kid	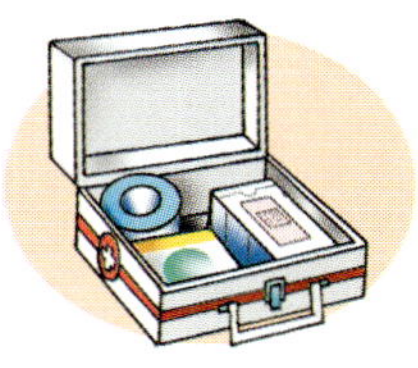	kit
o		cod	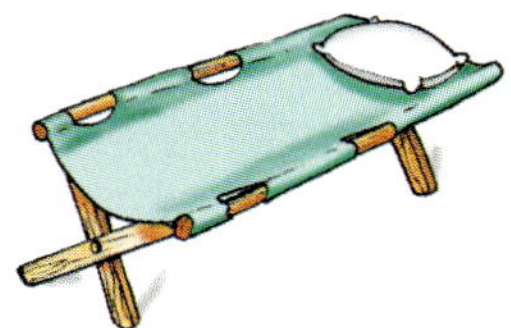	cot
u		cub		cut

The cat is on the cot with the cub.

a
e
i
o
u
m
n
f
s
h
j
r
ICE CREAM

	a	e	i	o	u
l	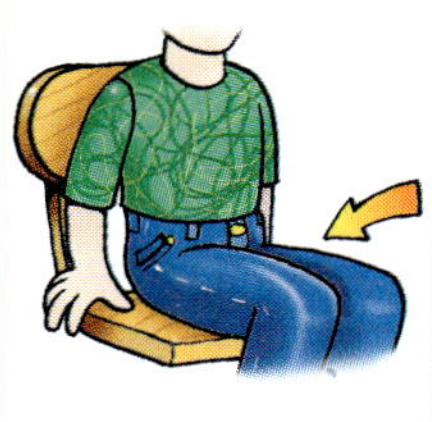		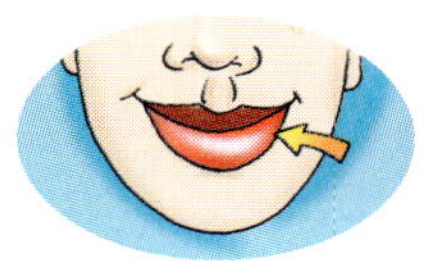		
b			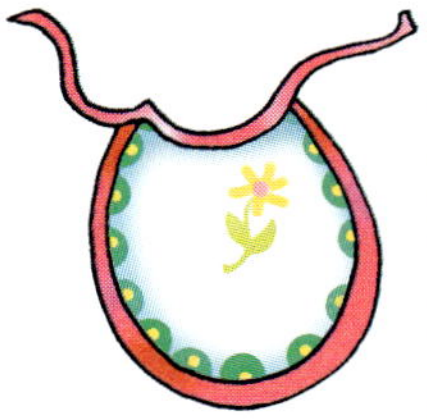	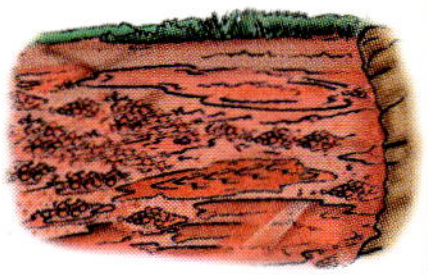	
p					
d					
t					
g					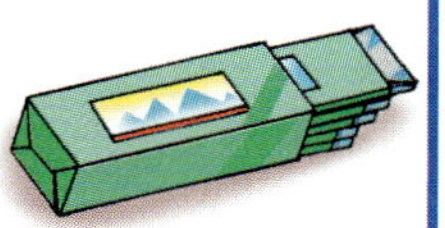
c, k		 Ken		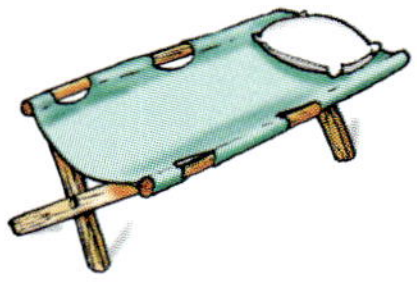	

	a	e	i	o	u
m	mat	men	mitt	mop	mug
n	nap	net	nit	nod	nut
f	fan	fed	fig	fog	fun
s	sad	set	sit	sob	sun
h	hat	hen	hit	hog	hug
j	jam	jet	jig	job	jug
r	rat	red	rip	rod	rug

	a	e	i	o	u
l	lap	leg	lip	log	luck
b	bat	bed	bib	bog	bus
p	pan	pen	pig	pot	pup
d	dad	den	dig	dot	duck
t	tag	ten	tip	top	tub
g	gas	get	gill	got	gum
c, k	cat	Ken	kid	cot	cut

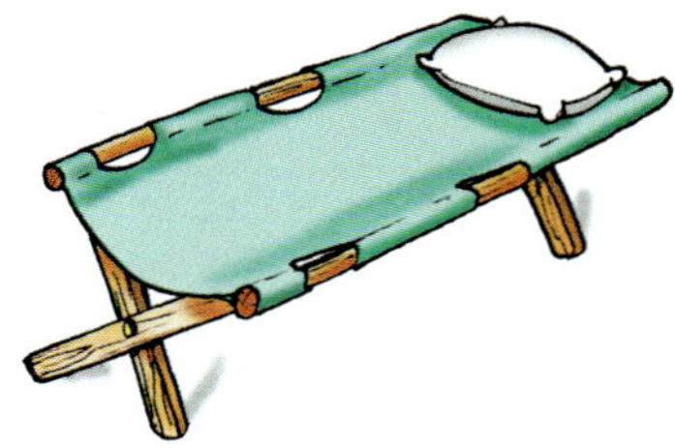

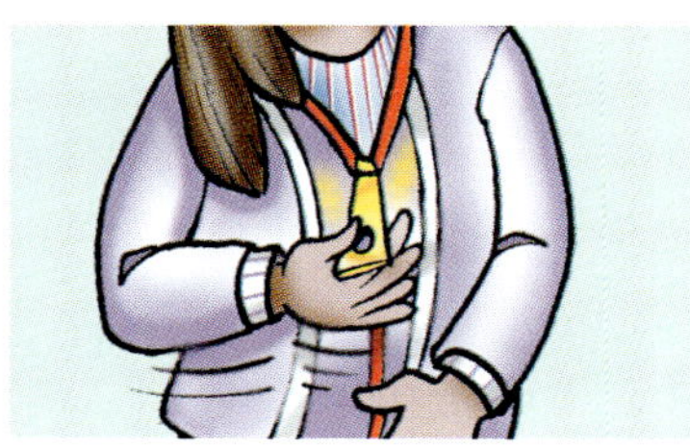

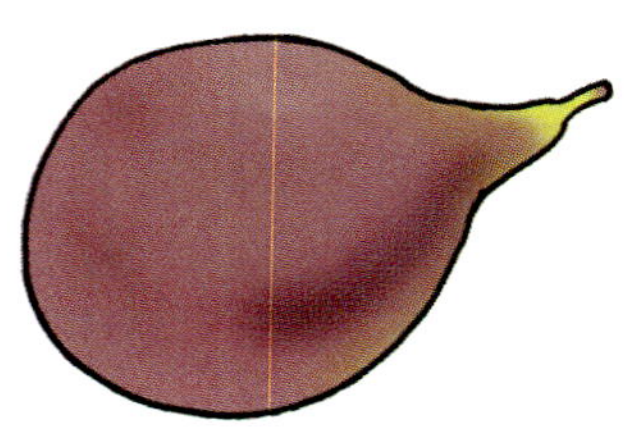

10

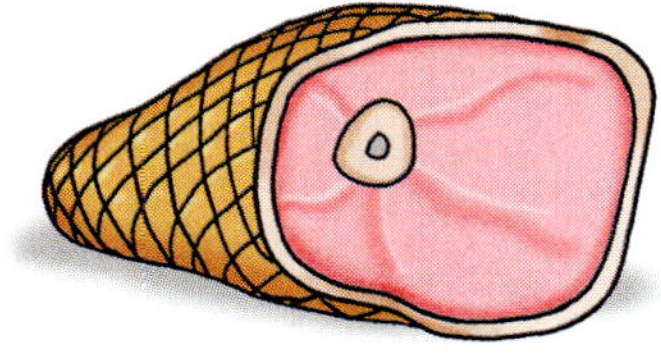
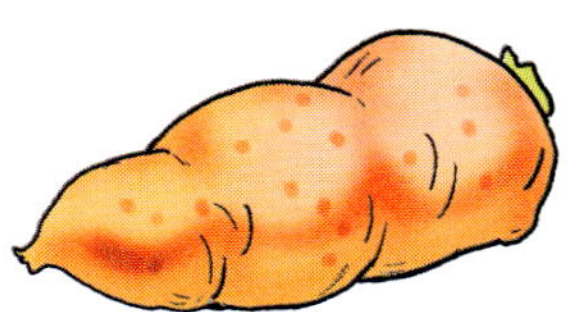

UNIT 3

DECODING & WORD RECOGNITION (1)

Initial Consonant Blends

cl, fl
cr, dr, fr, tr
sk, sl, sm, sp, st, sw

Final Consonant Blends

mp, nd, nt
lk, lt, ft
st, sk

Final Consonant *x*

Final Double Consonants

ss, ff, ll, ck

Initial Consonant *q(u)*

Initial Consonant Digraphs

sh, ch, th, wh

Final Consonant Digraphs

sh, th
ng, nk
ch, tch (Trigraph)

Review & Expansion

Distinguishing Initial & Final Sounds
Distinguishing Medial Sounds: Vocabulary Review Chart
Rhyming Words
Changes in Words: Adding Sounds
Changes in Words: Omitting Sounds
Changes in Words: Consonant & Vowel Substitutions
Changes in Words: Adding, Omitting, & Substituting Sounds

clam

clap

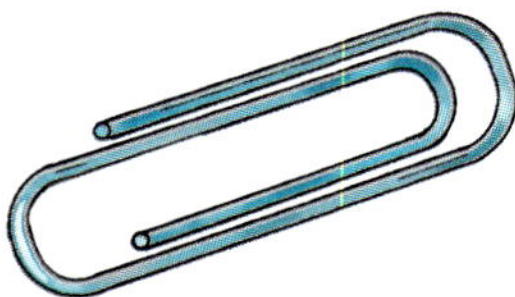

clip

club

flag

flap

flat

flip

The clam can clap.
The clip can flip.

cr

crab

crop

dr

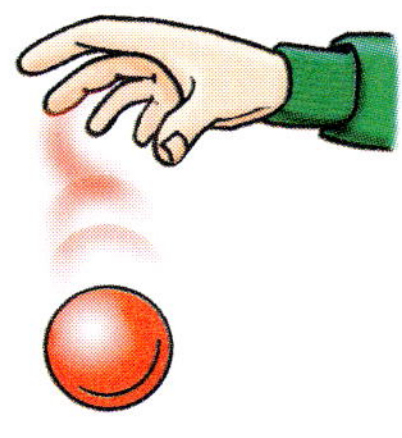

drop

drum

fr

Fran

frog

tr

trap

trot

The frog is in the trap with the crab.

sk

skin

skip

sl

slip

slug

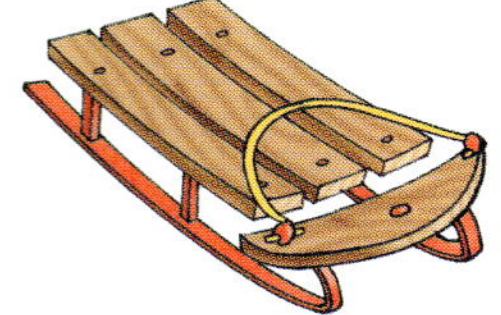

sled

slot

sm

smell

smog

The slug is on the sled.

sp

spin

spot

st

stem

step

stick

stop

sw

swap

swim

Swim and get the stick!

camp

lamp

ramp

stamp

bump

dump

hump

jump

Jump up and sit
on the hump.

nd

band

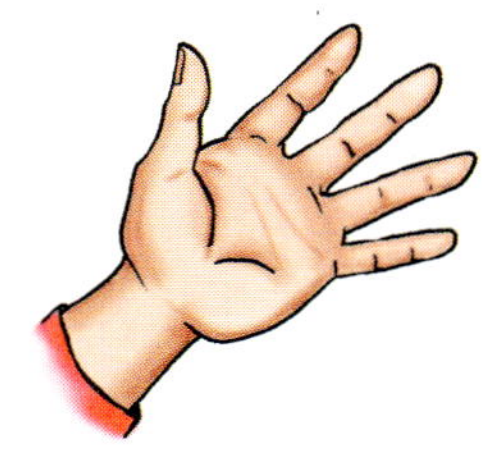
hand

sand

stand

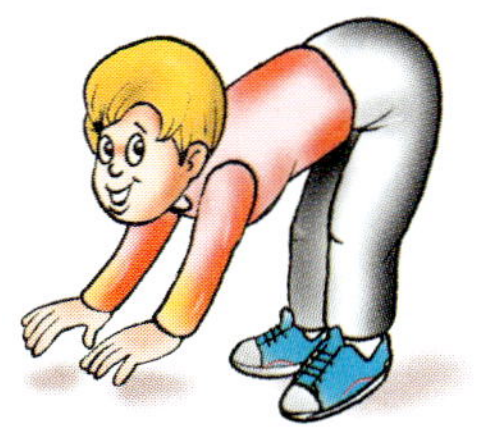
bend

mend

wind

pond

Stand in the sand
at the pond and
bend in the wind.

nt

ant

plant

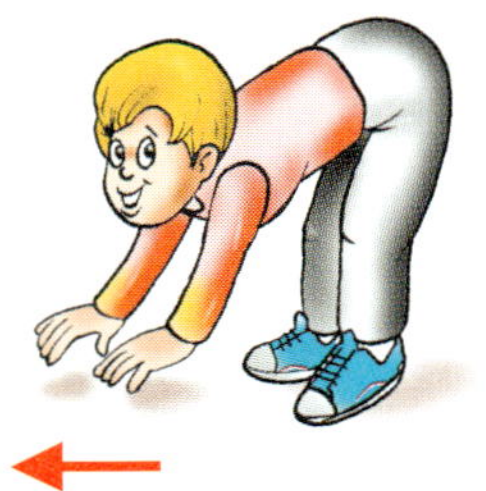

bent

dent

tent

went

print

hunt

The ant went in the tent.

elk

milk

lt

belt

melt

ft

raft

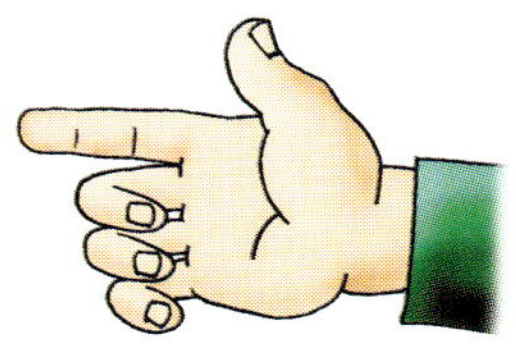

left

gift

lift

An elk with a gift
is on the raft.

st

fast

last

best

nest

rest

test

vest

west

Rest in the best
nest in the west.

st

fist

list

dust

crust

sk

ask

mask

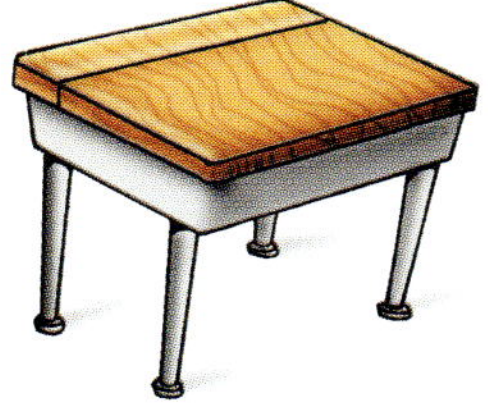

desk

disk

The disk is on the desk with the mask and the list.

 wax

 fix

 mix

 six

 box

 fox

Fix the box with the fox.

ss

class

glass

grass

dress

press

kiss

ff

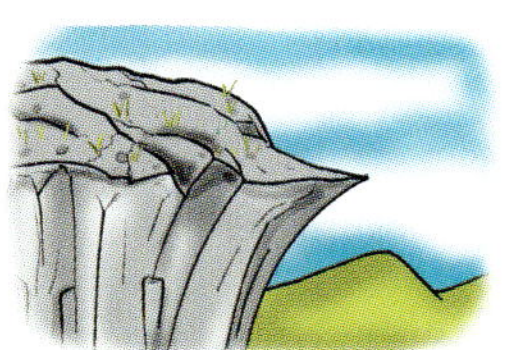

cliff

huff

puff

The class is in the grass on the cliff.

ll
bell
fell
Lemonade 25¢
sell
shell
smell
c a t
spell
tell
well

yell

The doll is with the ill gull at the well on the hill.

back

black

sack

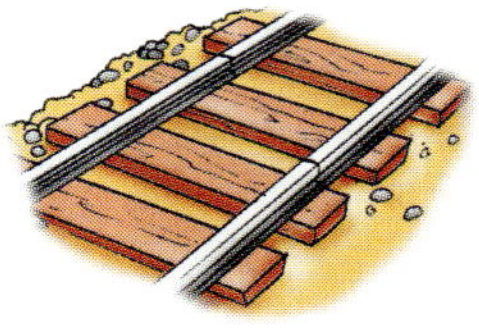

track

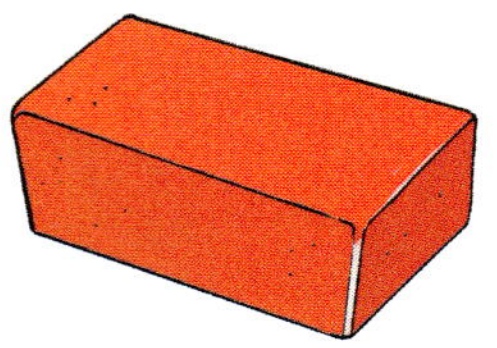

brick

kick

pick

sick

stick

trick

block

clock

lock

rock

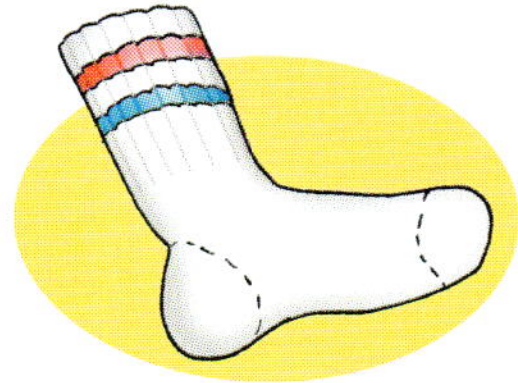

sock

duck

luck

truck

The duck did a trick with a block, a rock, a clock, and a black sack.

qu

 quack

 quick

 quill

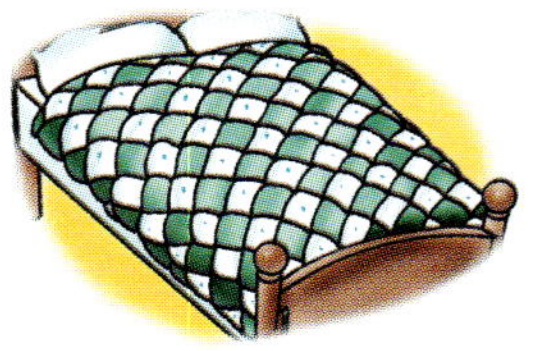 quilt

 quit

 quiz

---

Quack! Quack!

sh

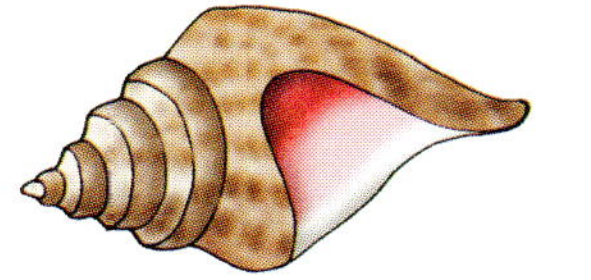

shell

shelf

shed

ship

shop

shut

The shell is with the ship on the shelf in the shop.

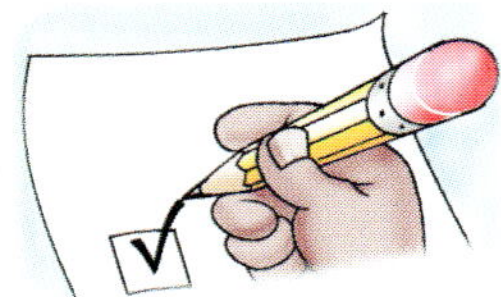
check

chest

chess

chin

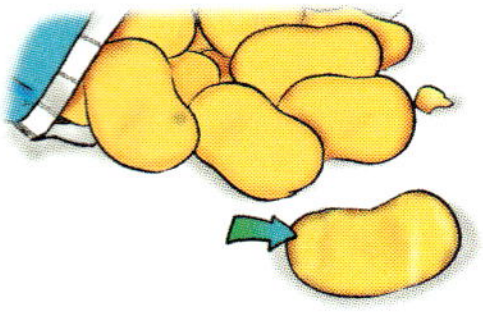
chip

chick

chimp

chop

The chimp and the chick chop and chop.

thank

think

thick

thin

this

that

when

which

"Which is thin and which is thick?"

"This is thin and that is thick."

crash

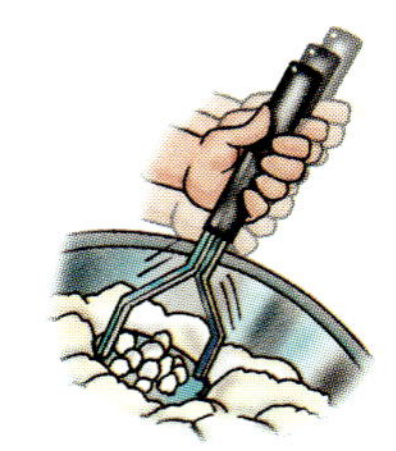

mash

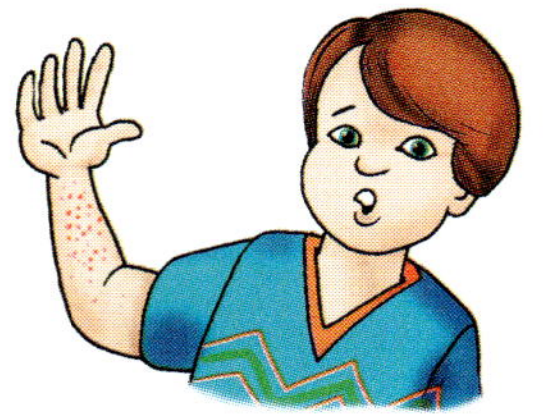

rash

trash

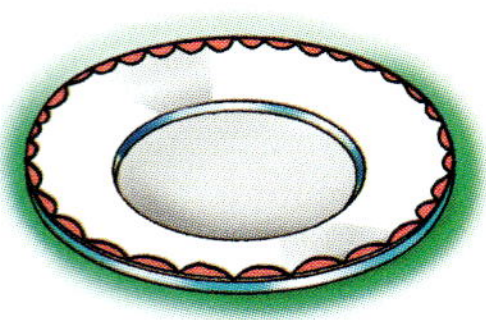

dish

fish

wish

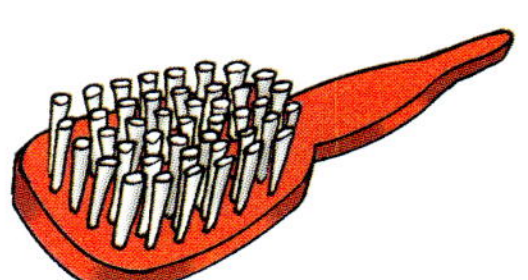

brush

The fish in this dish is fresh.

 bath

 math

 path

 Beth

 Seth

 with

---

Beth is with Seth
in math.

ng

bang

fang

hang

rang

sang

bring

king

ring

ring

sing

sling

sting

swing

thing

wing

ding dong

ping pong

King Kong

The king sang on the swing.

bank

blank

crank

drank

tank

thank

blink

drink

pink

rink

sink

stink

think

wink

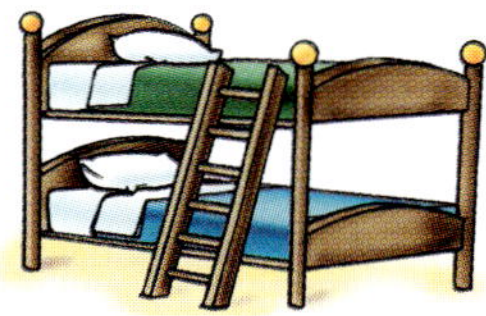

bunk

junk

skunk

trunk

Hank and Frank think
a skunk is in the bunk.

rich

which

ranch

branch

inch

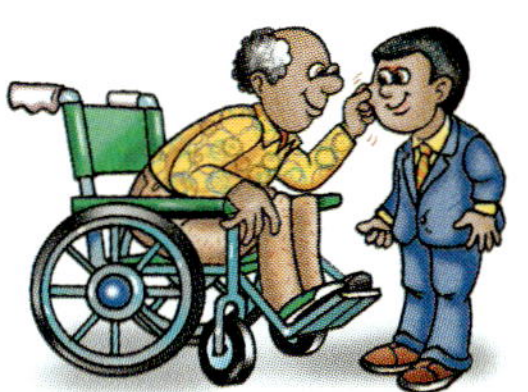

pinch

bench

lunch

Sit on the bench and have lunch at the ranch.

catch

patch

sketch

itch

ditch

pitch

switch

Dutch

Pitch and catch in a ditch.

DISTINGUISHING INITIAL & FINAL SOUNDS (1)

m   m

s   s

b   b

t   t

n   n

p 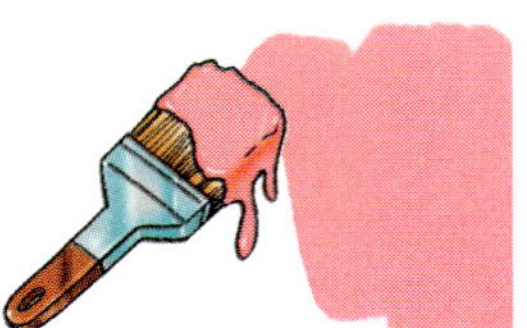  p

f			f
g			g
l			l
d			d
k			ck
ch			ch

b

b

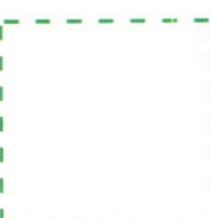

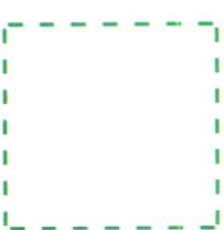

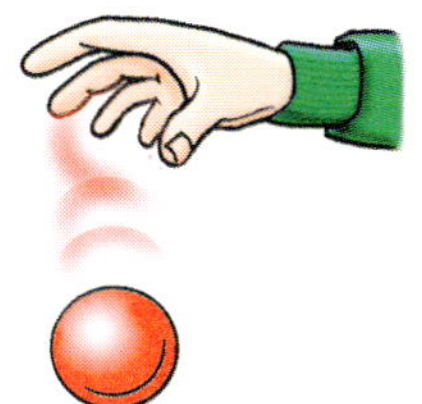

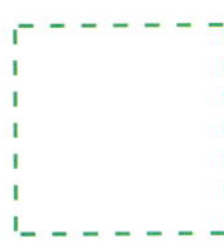

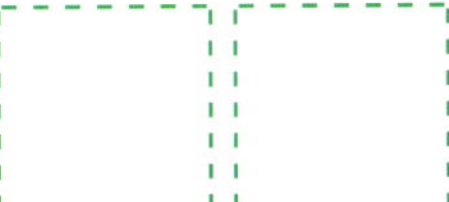

5 3
3 +4
8

	a	e	i	o	u
m					
n			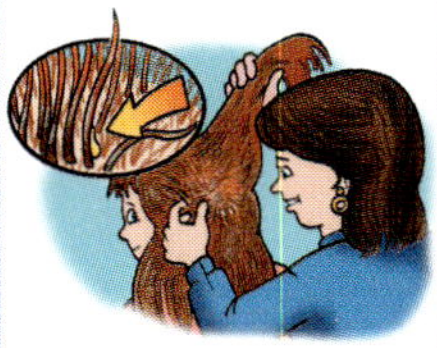		
f					
s			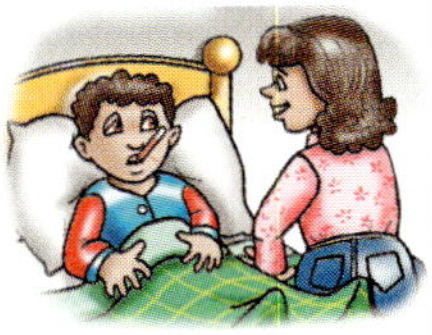	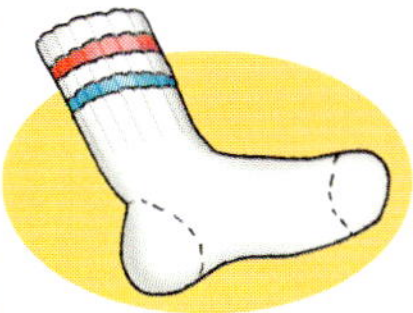	
h	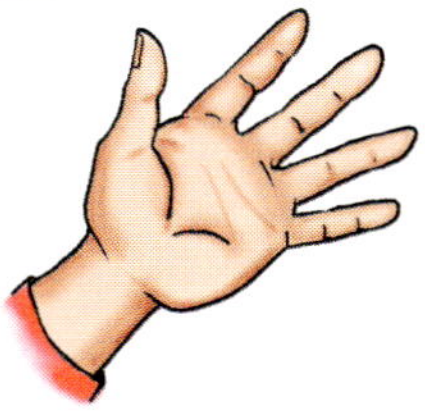				
j					
r					

	a	e	i	o	u
l		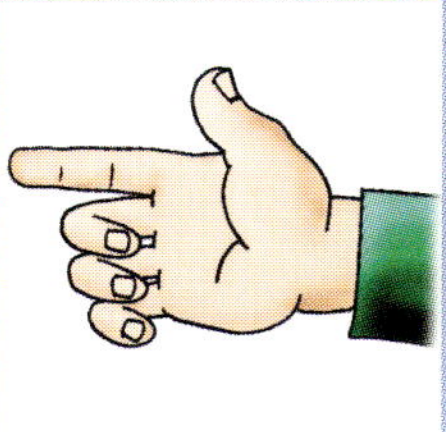			
b			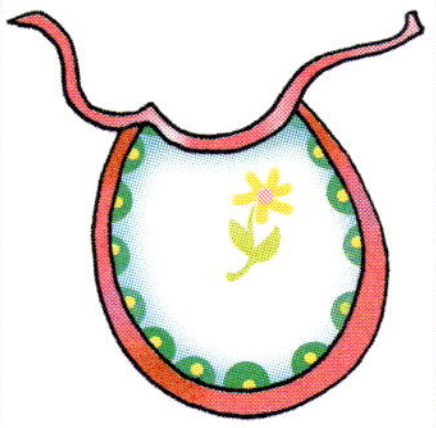		
p					
d					
t					
g					
c, k		 Ken			

RHYMING WORDS (1)

6

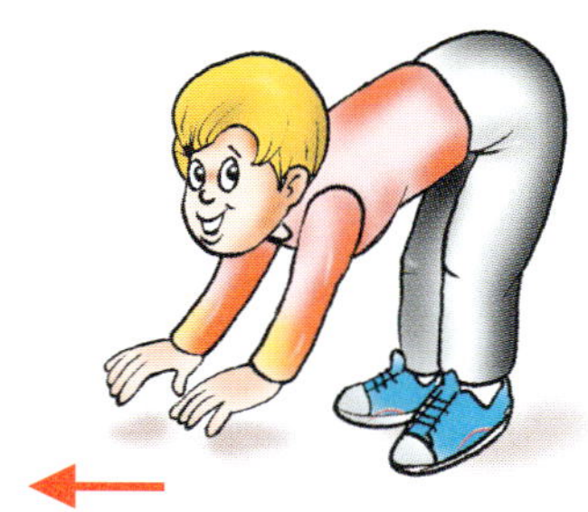

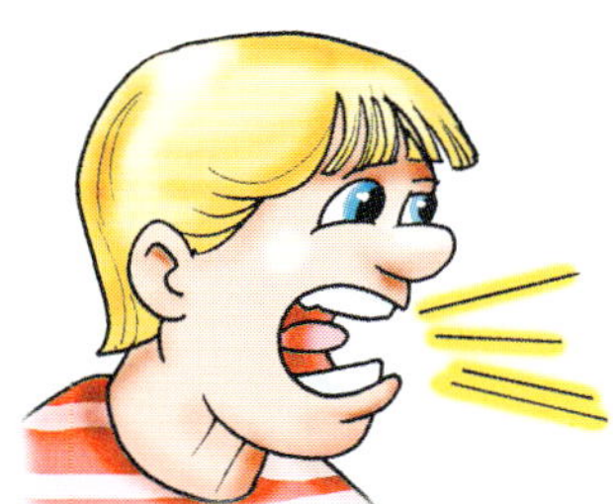

Lemonade 25¢

27
62

5
3
3
+4
8

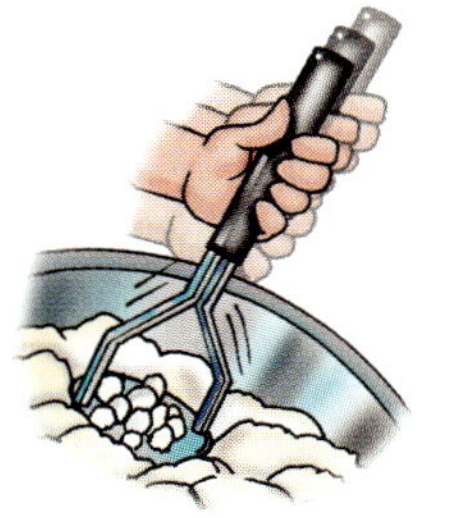

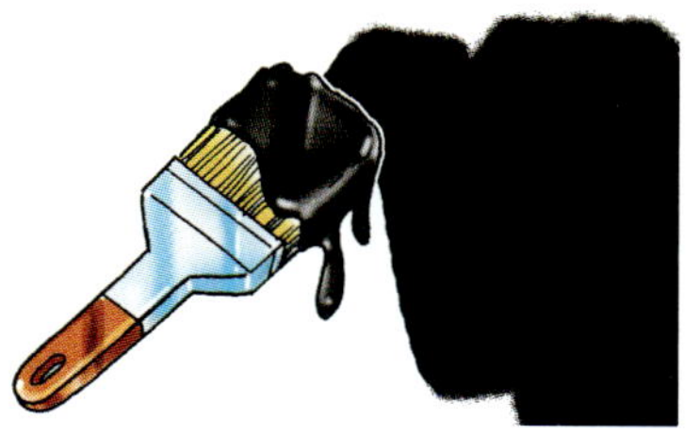

lock    clock

wing    swing

back    black

sick    stick

thin   think

sand   stand

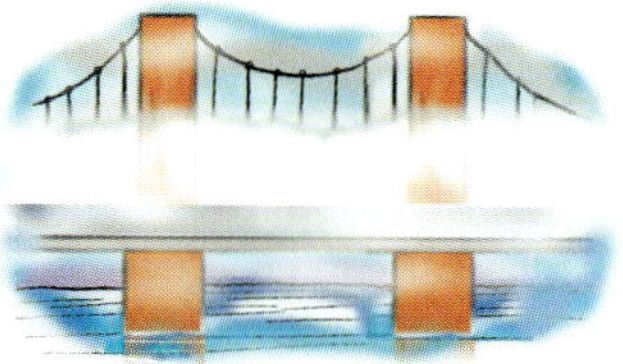

This is

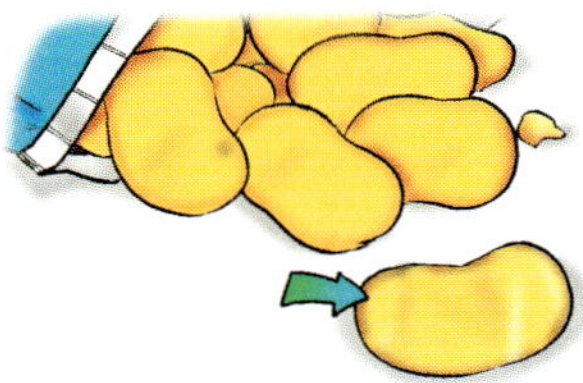

stop	top
pitch	itch
trick	tick
pinch	inch
mask	ask
crash	rash

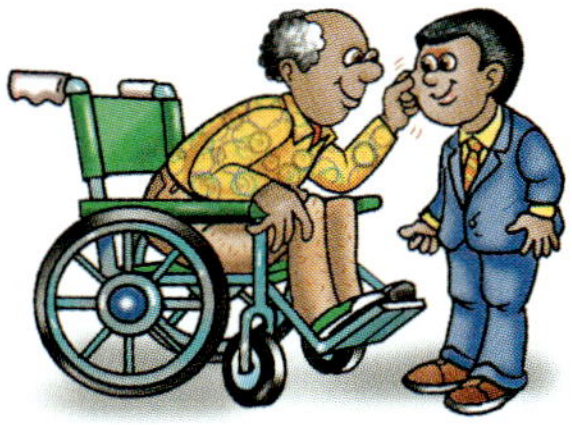

10

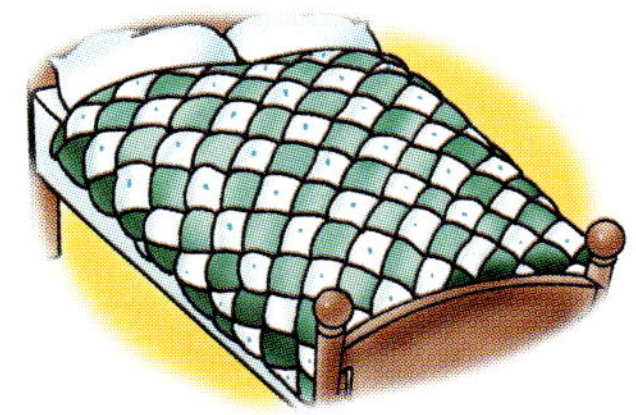

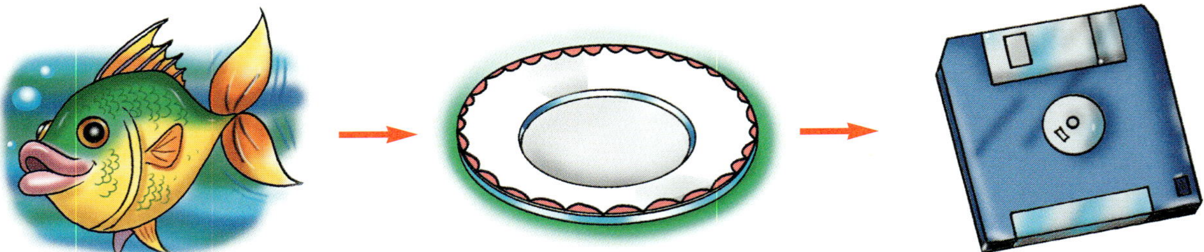

c a t
4
5
6

This is

UNIT 4

DECODING & WORD RECOGNITION (2)

Long Vowel Word Families

a_e, i_e, o_e, u_e
ee, ea
Final Long Vowels *e* & *o*
Long Vowel Word Families with *ace, ice*
y as a Vowel
Long Vowels with *ld, ll, lt, nd*
Distinguishing Short & Long Vowels

Vowel Digraphs

ay, ai
oa, oe, ow
oo, ou, ew, ue

R-Controlled Vowels

ar, ir, ur, er, or

Two-Syllable Words

Two-Syllable Words with *y* as a Vowel

Review & Expansion

Rhyming Words
Changes in Words

bake

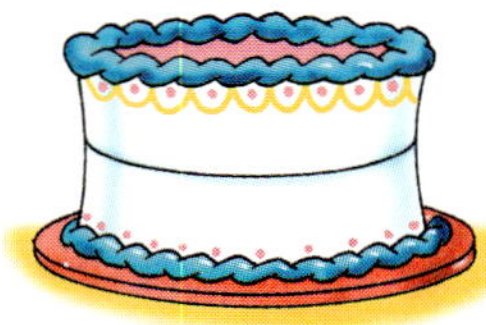

cake

rake

snake

game

name

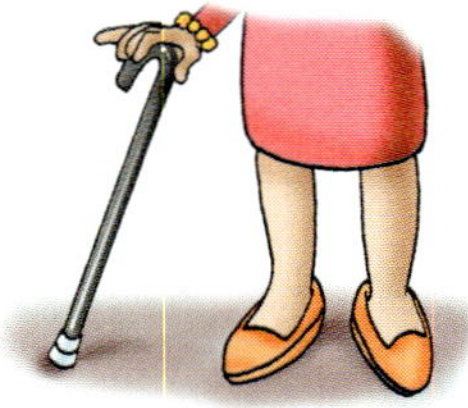

cane

lane

mane

plane

cape

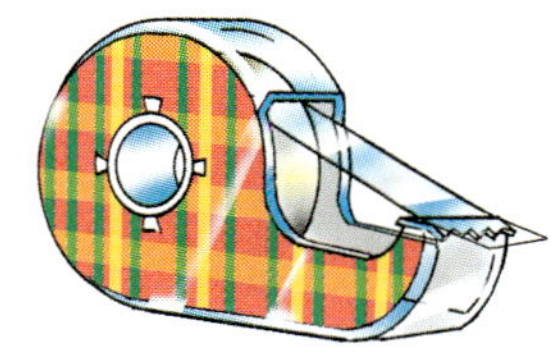

tape

ate

gate

plate

skate

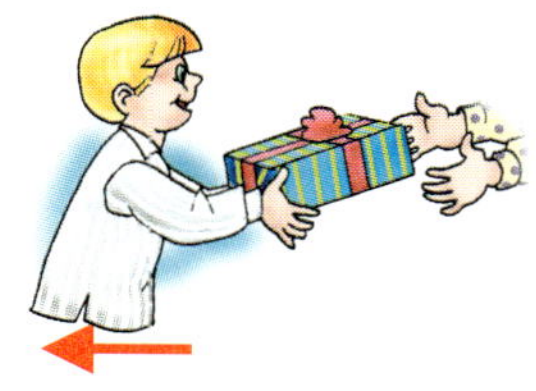

gave

save

A snake in a cape ate the cake on a plate.

hide

ride

side

slide

bike

hike

dime

time

nine

pine

pipe

wipe

bite

kite

dive

drive

five

hive

The kite is in the pine with the hive.

globe

robe

rode

broke

smoke

hole

mole

pole

stole

dome

home

bone

cone

note

vote

stove

drove

A mole in a robe is
at home in a hole.

cube

tube

rude

duke

Luke

mule

rule

dune

June

tune

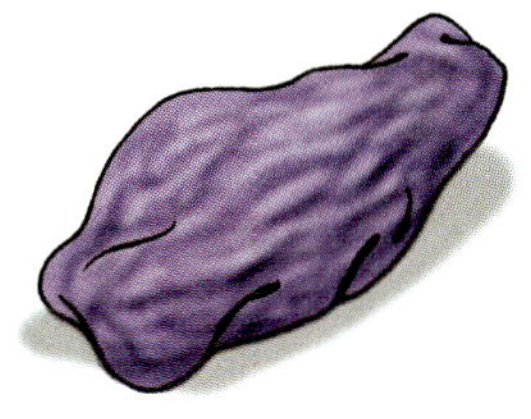

prune

cute

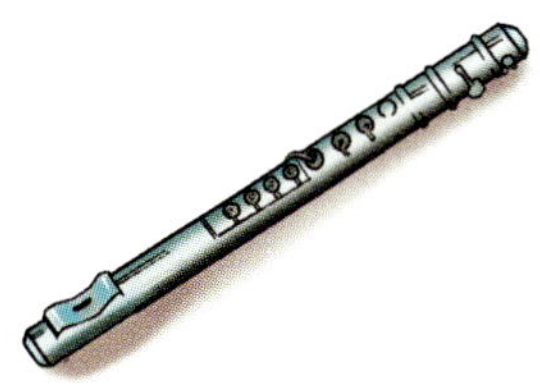

flute

A duke with a flute
is on a cute mule
on a dune.

man

mane

bit

bite

not

note

tub

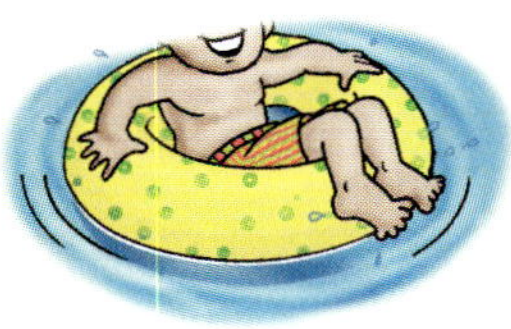

tube

tap

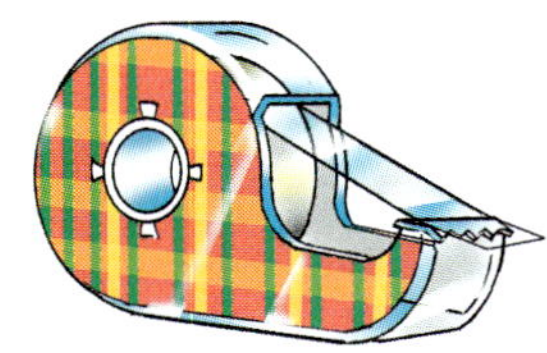

tape

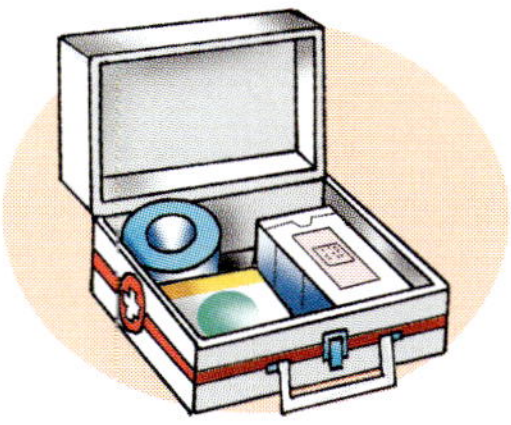

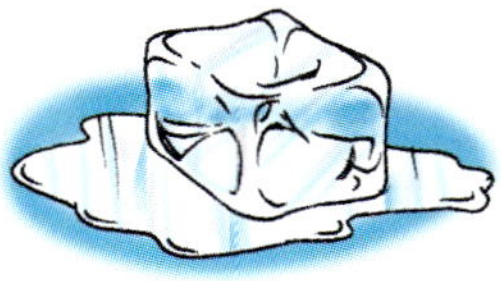

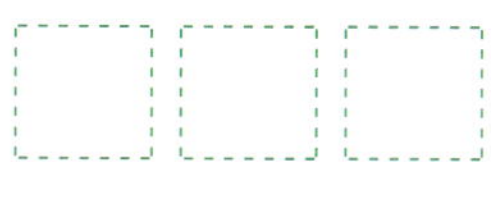

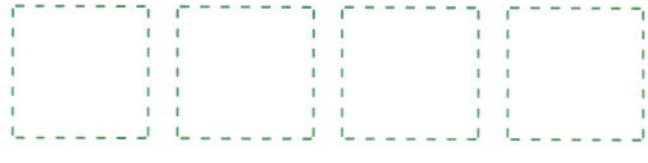

bee

see

three

tree

feed

seed

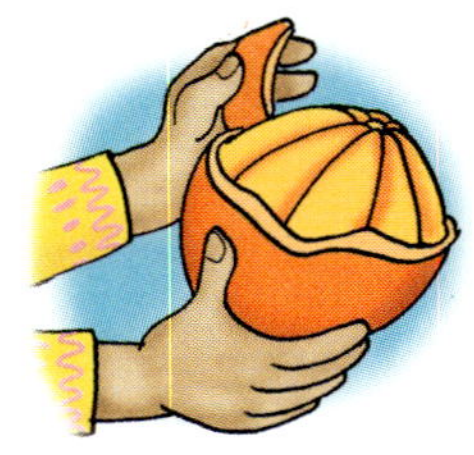

peel

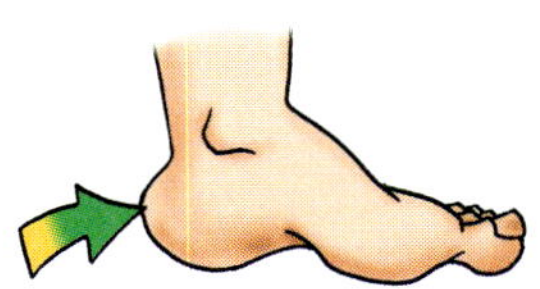

heel

green

queen

jeep

sheep

sleep

sweep

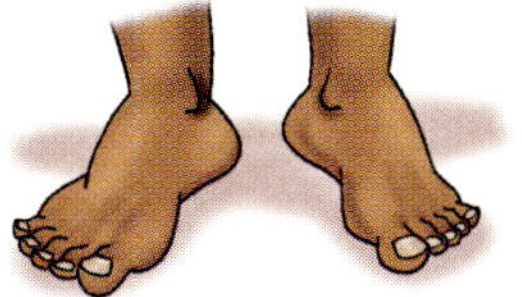

feet

meet

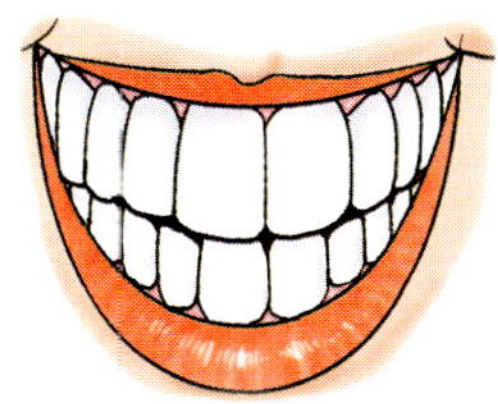

teeth

The queen is in a
green jeep with
three sheep.

ea

pea

sea

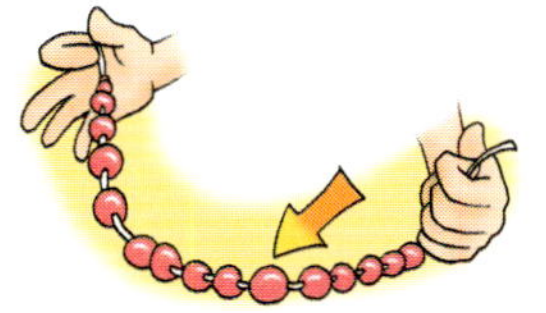
bead

read

meal

seal

dream

team

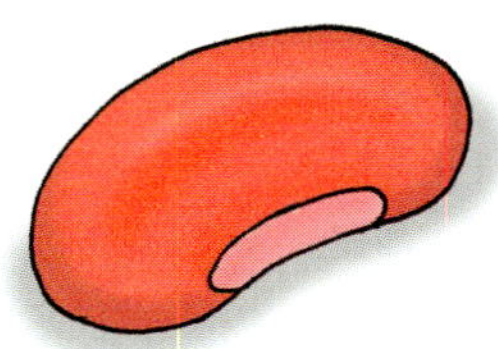
bean

clean

eat

beat

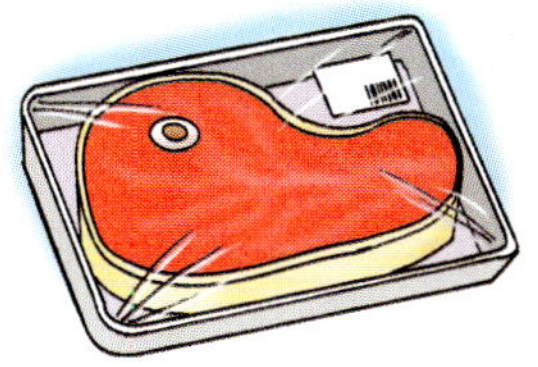

meat

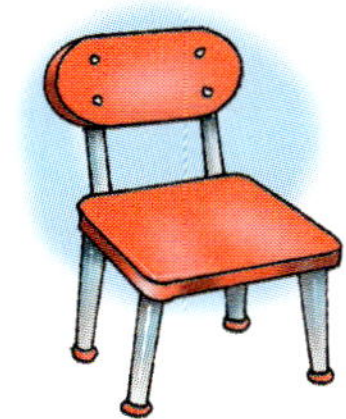

seat

peach

teach

leaf

east

Eat a meal with a seal.

he

she

me

we

go

no

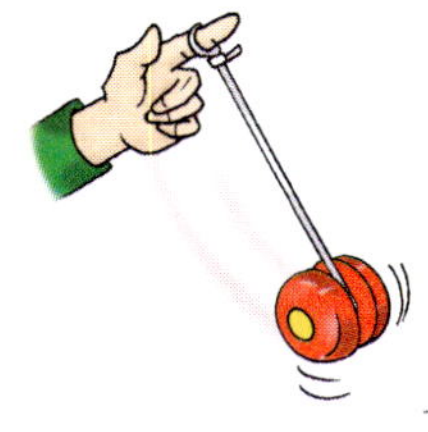

yo-yo

ace

brace

face

space

race

ice

ice

mice

rice

slice

y

happy

penny

bunny

windy

baby

tiny

pony

sleepy

The tiny bunny
is sleepy.

y

cry  dry

fly  fly

fry  my

sky  why

Why did the fly cry?

ay

clay

day

gray

hay

jay

May

play

say

Kay and Jay play
with the gray clay.

rain

train

chain

paint

pail

sail

tail

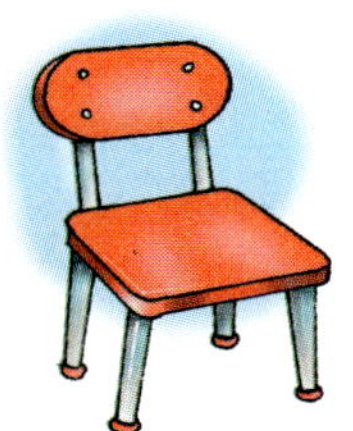

chair

Sail in the rain.

oa

boat

coat

goat

float

road

toad

loaf

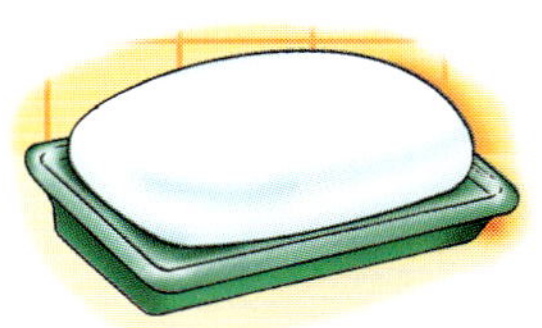
soap

---

oe

hoe

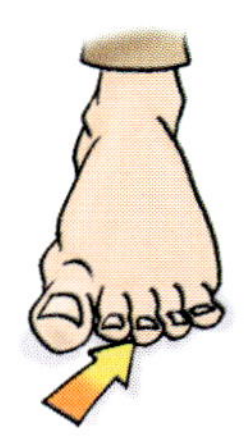
toe

ow

bow

blow

crow

grow

low

row

snow

throw

The crow and the toad throw snow at the goat in the road.

oo

zoo

boot

moon

spoon

pool

stool

broom

tooth

---

ou

soup

you

ew

blew

drew

flew

grew

new

threw

ue

blue

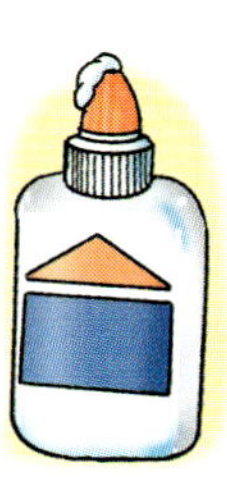

glue

The new blue spoon is in the soup.

ld

old

cold

fold

gold

hold

sold

told

child

wild

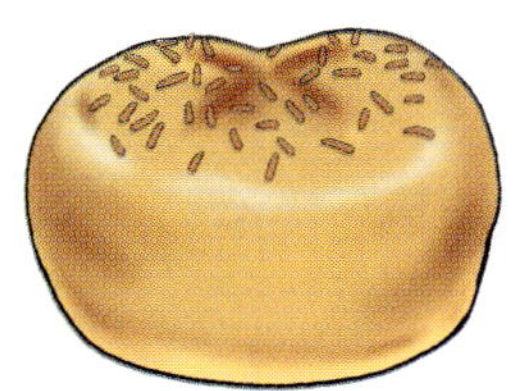

roll

toll

lt

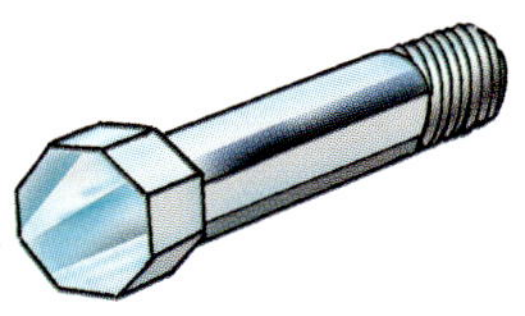

bolt

colt

nd

blind

find

kind

wind

The child and the colt find the gold.

car

far

jar

star

card

yard

bark

dark

park

shark

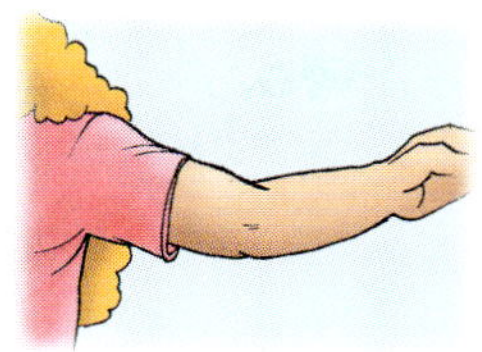
arm

farm

barn

yarn

harp

sharp

cart

smart

Bark in the dark in the yard.

ir

bird

girl

shirt

skirt

stir

first

---

ur

curl

turn

hurt

church

er

herd

fern

or

fork

storm

corn

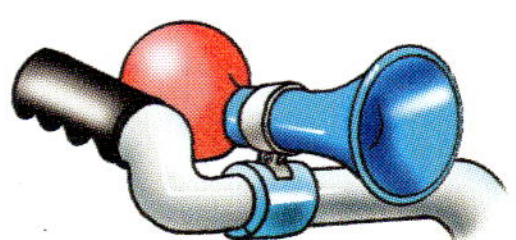

horn

short

north

The girl and the bird
stir the corn with a fork.

RHYMING WORDS (1)

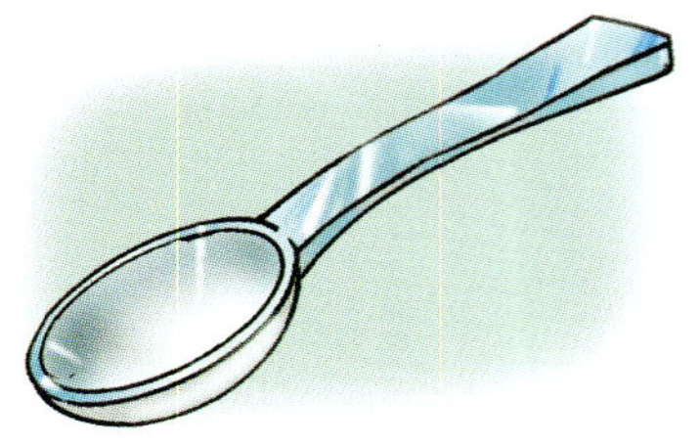
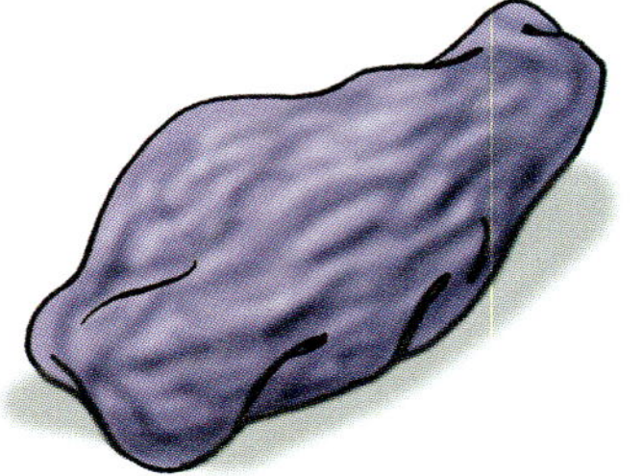

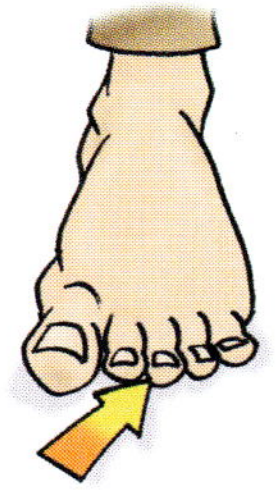

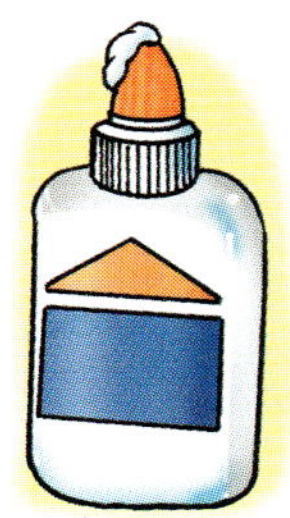

10

12

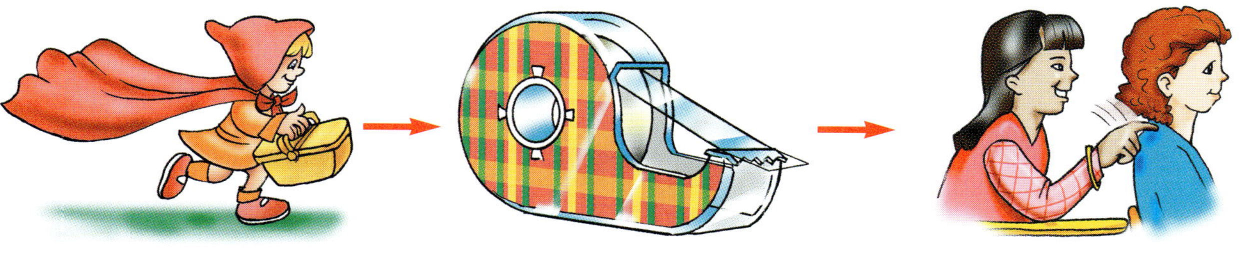

CHANGES IN WORDS (3)

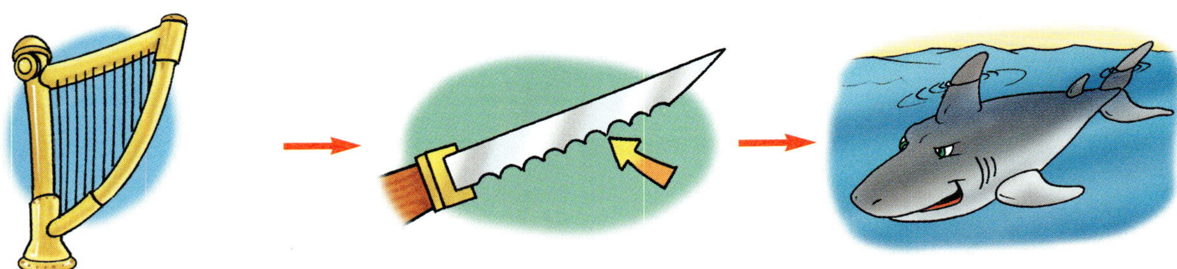

UNIT 5

DECODING & WORD RECOGNITION (3)

Vowel Diphthongs

ou, ow
oi, oy

Vowel Sounds & Spelling Patterns

aw, au, o
all
ore, oar, our, oor
oo, u
o, ea

Complex Word Families

igh, ight; ought, aught; eigh, eight

Syllabication

Medial Consonants (VCV: Vowel–Consonant–Vowel)
Double Medial Consonants (VCCV: Vowel–Consonant–Consonant–Vowel)
Different Medial Consonants (VCCV: Vowel–Consonant–Consonant–Vowel)
Two-Syllable Words with Final *le*

Silent Letters

k, w, h, l, t, b

Plural Nouns

Regular Plurals (Inflections *s, es*)
Plurals with Spelling Changes (*y* to *i*; *f* to *v*)
Irregular Plurals

Initial Consonant Blends

scr, spl, spr, str, squ

Root Words & Inflections

Verbs with Inflections *s, ed, ing*
Inflections *s, ed, ing* with Spelling Changes

Suffixes

Nouns with Suffixes *er, or*

Consonant Sounds & Spelling Patterns

Consonant *s* = *z*
Consonants *ph, gh* = *f*
Soft Consonant *g*

Common Irregular Sight Words

come, give, said, have, some, none, was, were

Review & Expansion

Rhyming Words

cloud

shout

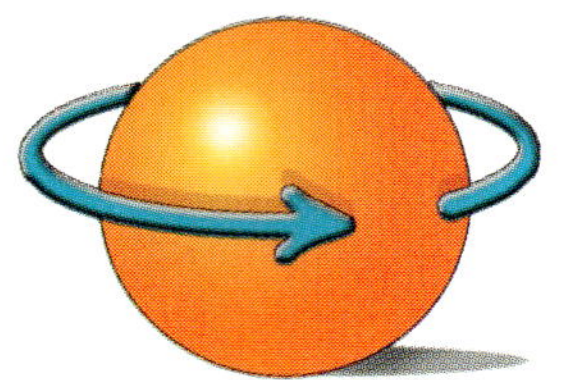

round

count

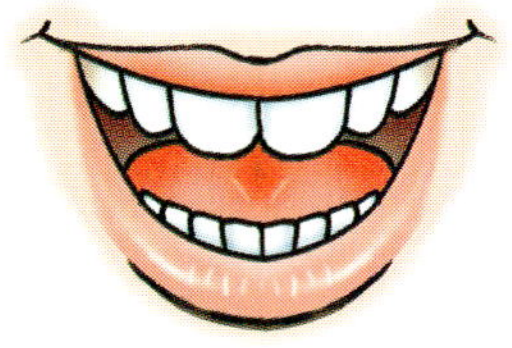

mouth

south

house

mouse

our

flour

ow

bow

cow

how

owl

brown

clown

down

town

How did a cow, an owl, and a brown mouse get in our house?

oi

oil

boil

foil

soil

coin

point

oy

boy

toy

The boy is in the soil with the toy.

aw

draw

saw

au

Paul

sauce

o

off

dog

long

song

Paul saw a dog
on a long log.

ball

call

fall

fall

hall

tall

wall

small

The small ball hit the wall in the hall.

ore 

score  store

---

oar 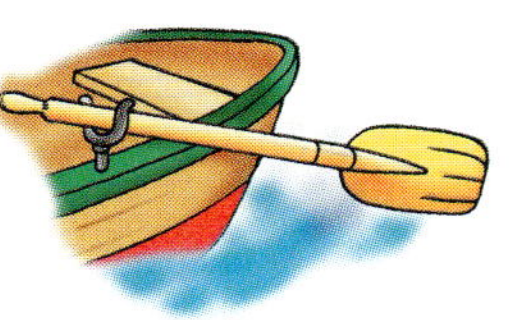 oar  roar

---

our  four  pour

---

oor  door  floor

---

Roar at the door
in the store.

book

brook

cook

hook

look

took

good

wood

wool

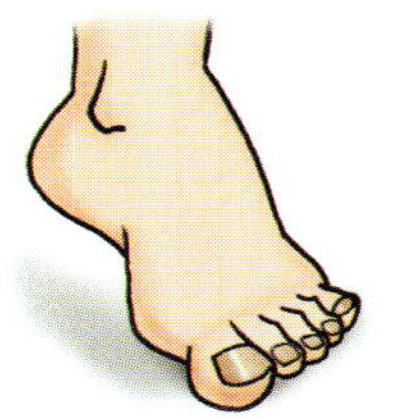

foot

u

bull

full

pull

bush

push

put

The bull took the
wood and put it
in the brook.

high

sigh

ight

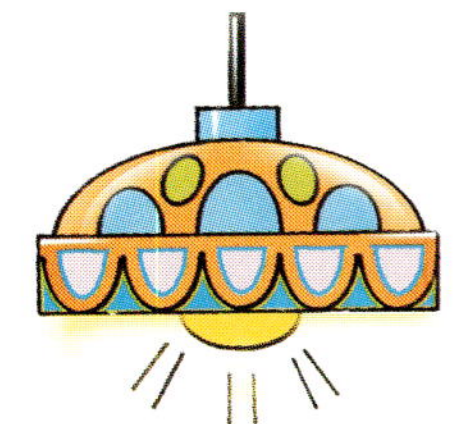

light

night

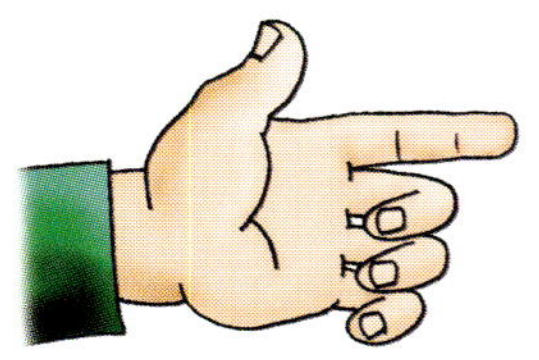

right

bright

ought

brought

thought

aught

caught

taught

eigh

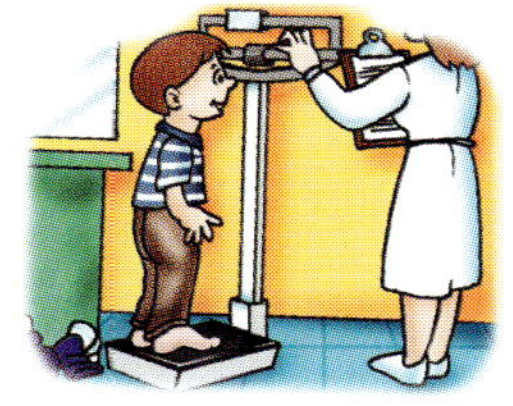

weigh

sleigh

eight

eight

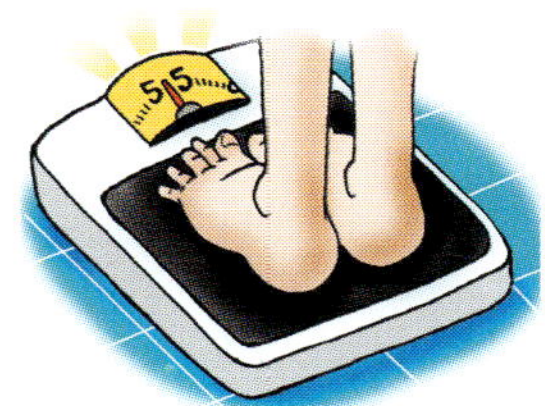

weight

eighty

cabin

camel

wagon

dragon

planet

shadow

seven

present

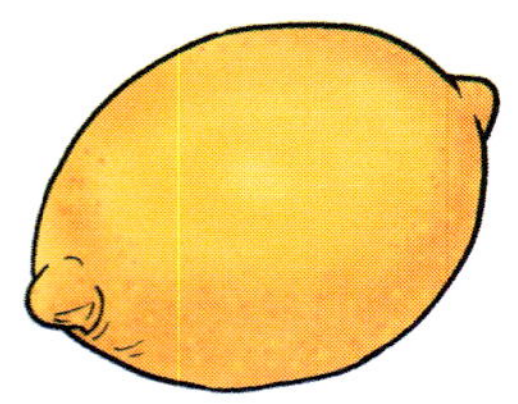

lemon

flower

paper

baker

over

broken

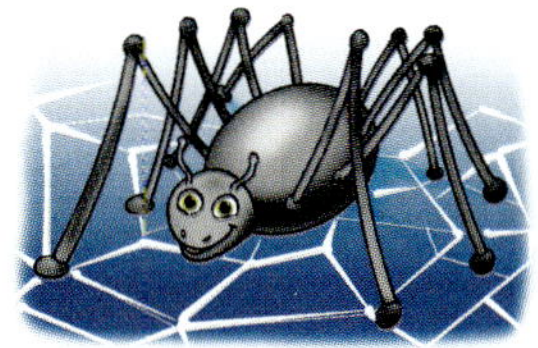

spider

Friday

sneaker

crayon

The wagon with the dragon is broken.

rabbit

ladder

yellow

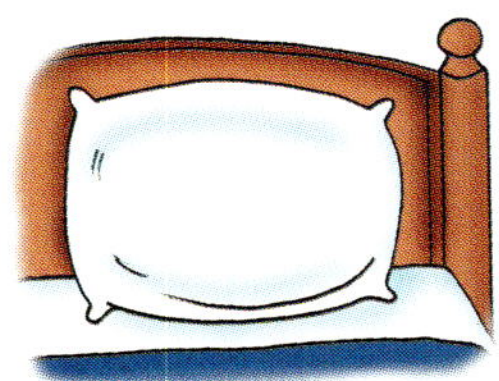
pillow

dollar

follow

hammer

summer

dinner

muffin

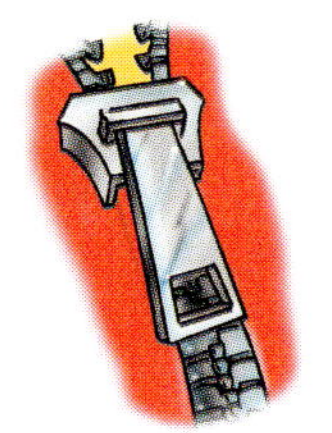

zipper

puppet

supper

letter

kitten

mitten

butter

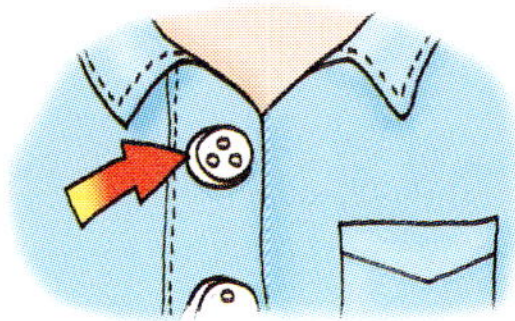

button

The rabbit and the kitten had a muffin with butter for dinner.

jacket

chicken

doctor

tractor

fifteen

fifty

pencil

princess

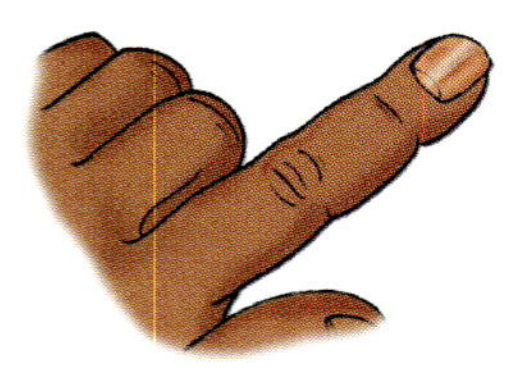

finger

blanket

window

under

Sunday

winter

dirty

sister

father

angry

The princess is angry at the chicken under the window.

mother

brother

honey

money

Monday

shovel

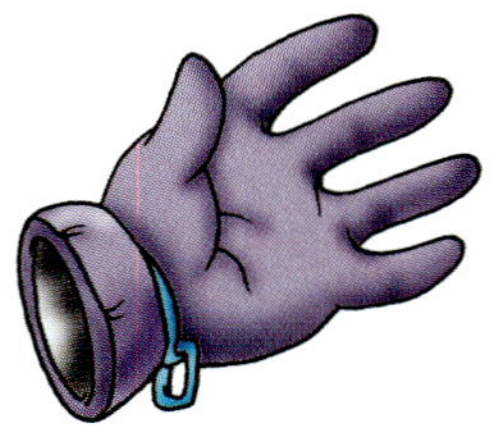

glove

above

monkey

donkey

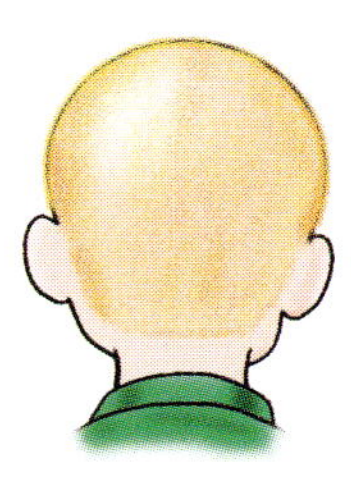

head

bread

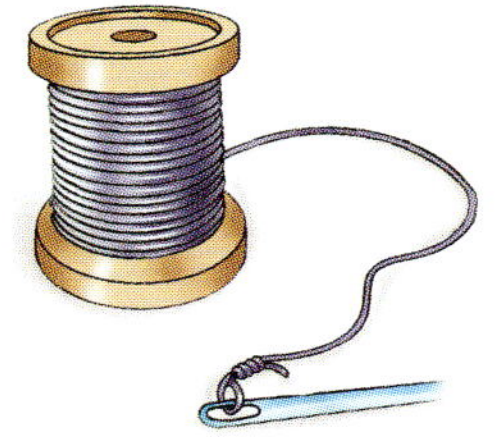

thread

heavy

feather

weather

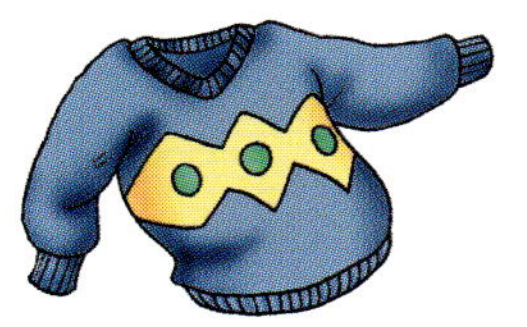

sweater

breakfast

The monkey and the donkey eat bread with honey for breakfast.

apple

bubble

middle

puddle

little

puzzle

turtle

purple

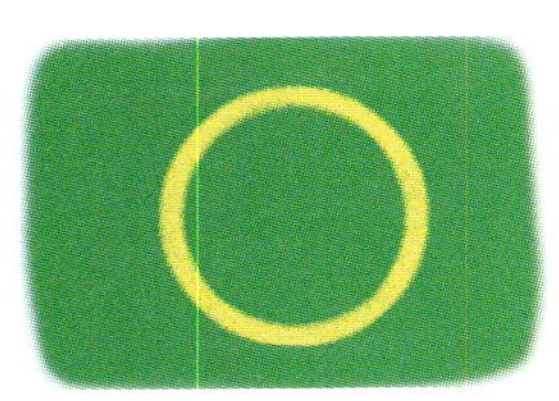

circle

tickle

needle

steeple

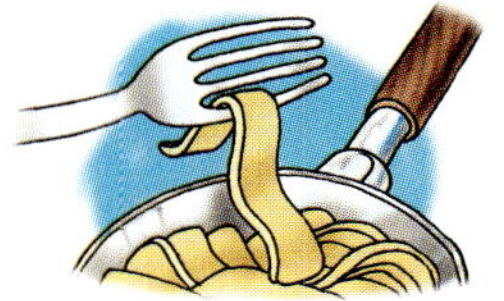

noodle

poodle

beetle

eagle

table

cradle

The turtle and the beetle sit in the middle of a little puddle.

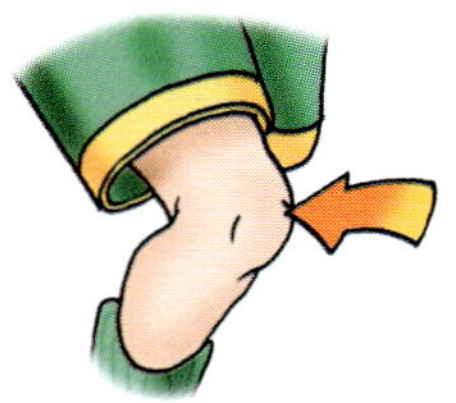
knee

knife

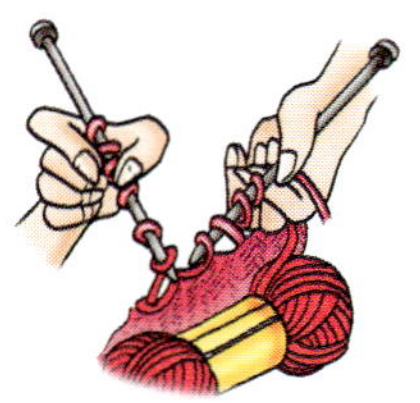
knit

knock

---

w

wrap

write

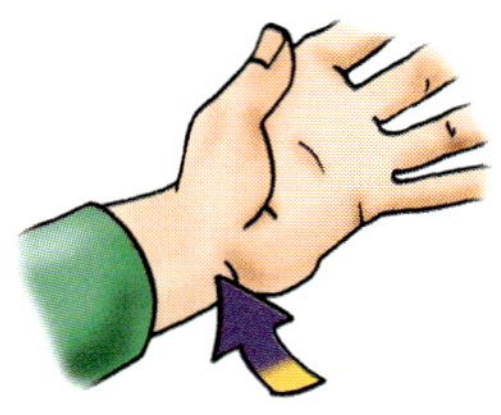
wrist

wrong

---

h

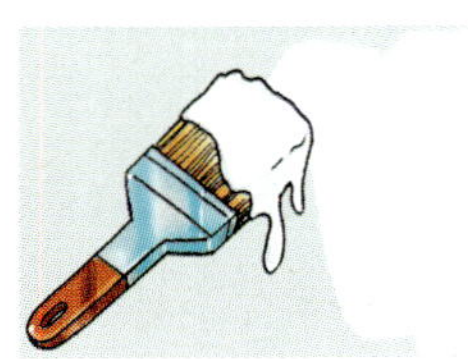
white

wheel

wheat

whale

l

 talk

 walk

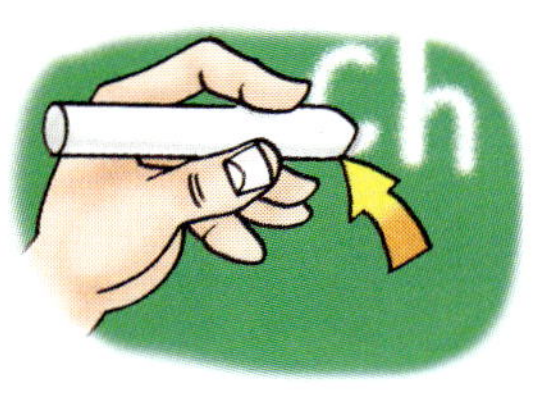

chalk

 calf

 half

---

t

  listen

 castle

---

b

 lamb

 comb

 climb

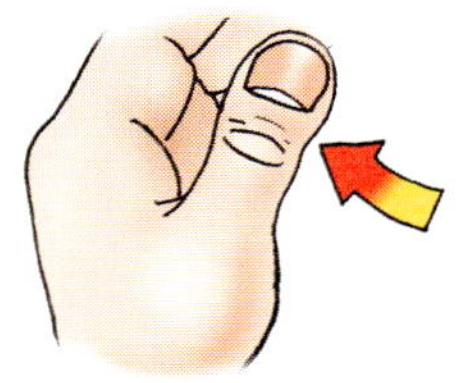 thumb

map
maps

book
books

seat
seats

bike
bikes

pen
pens

pencil
pencils

ruler
rulers

globe
globes

glass
glasses

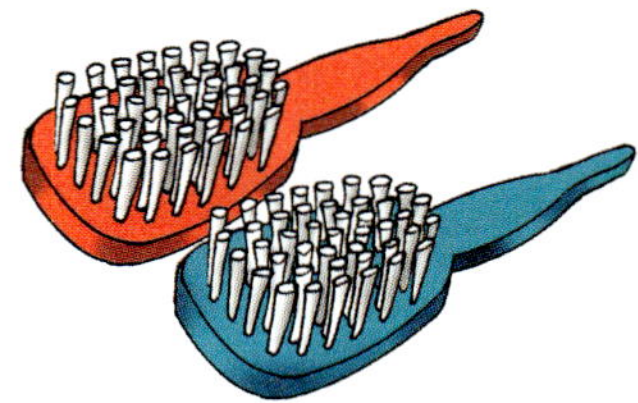

brush
brushes

watch
watches

box
boxes

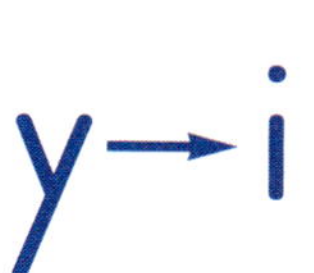

penny
pennies

puppy
puppies

baby
babies

fly
flies

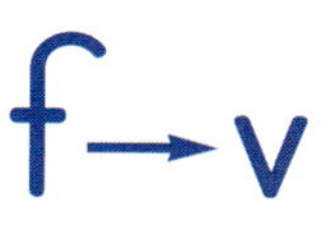

leaf
leaves

loaf
loaves

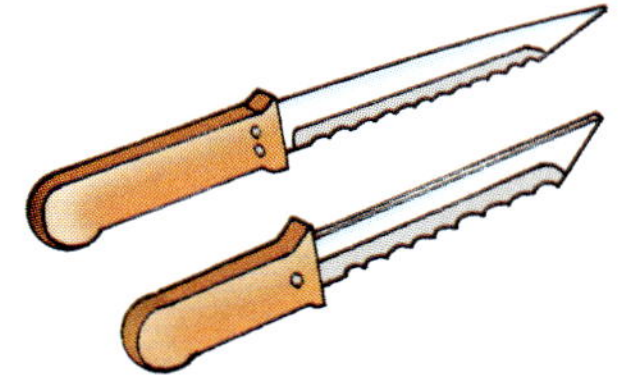

knife
knives

wolf
wolves

elf
elves

shelf
shelves

calf
calves

half
halves

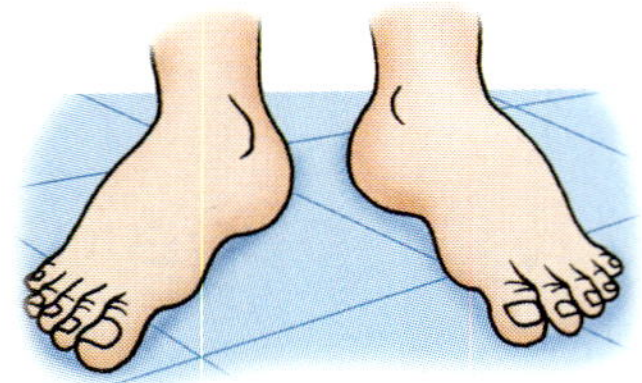

foot
feet

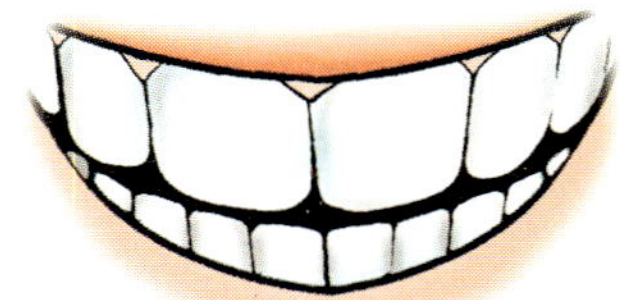

tooth
teeth

goose
geese

mouse
mice

man
men

woman
women

child
children

fish
fish

sheep
sheep

deer
deer

scr

scratch

scream

---

spl

splash

split

---

spr

spray

spring

---

str

straw

street

stretch

string

---

squ

square

squirrel

		s	ed	ing
	cook	cooks	cooked	cooking
	work	works	worked	working
	clean	cleans	cleaned	cleaning
	play	plays	played	playing
	brush	brushes	brushed	brushing
	add	adds	added	adding

	s	ed	ing
study	studies y → i	studied y → i	studying
bake	bakes	baked	baking e̸
shop	shops	shopped p → pp	shopping p → pp
jog	jogs	jogged g → gg	jogging g → gg

I play. She works.
He studies.
Yesterday we shopped.
Now we're jogging.

teach
teacher

farm
farmer

sing
singer

paint
painter

act
actor

conduct
conductor

bake
baker

dance
dancer

jog
jogger

shop
shopper

swim
swimmer

win
winner

hose

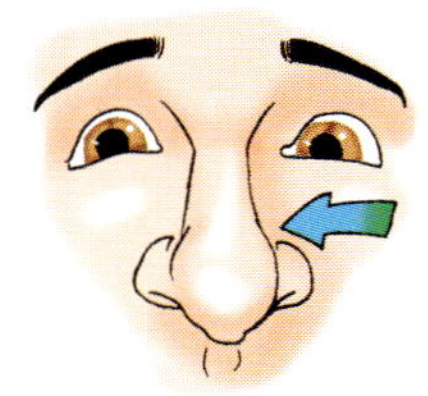

nose

rose

close

these

those

cheese

choose

please

has

easy

busy

phone

photo

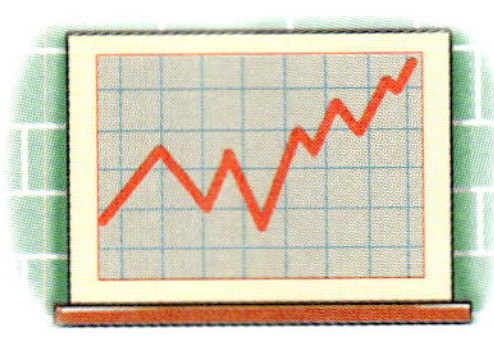

graph

dolphin

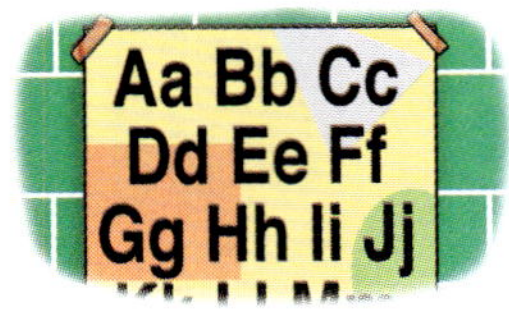

alphabet

elephant

---

gh

laugh

cough

---

g

giant

giraffe

large

orange

come

give

said

have

some

none

was

were

"Come and give me some oranges," said the giant.

"But I have none," said the elephant as he laughed.

1
+2
4

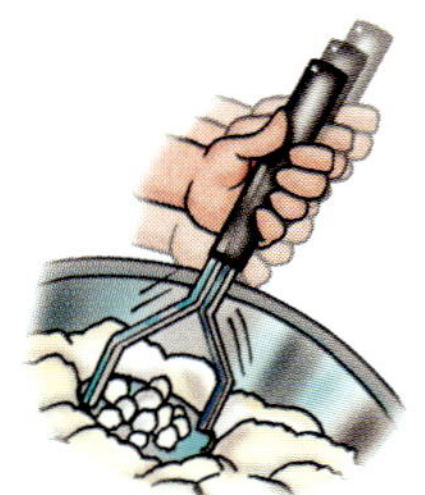

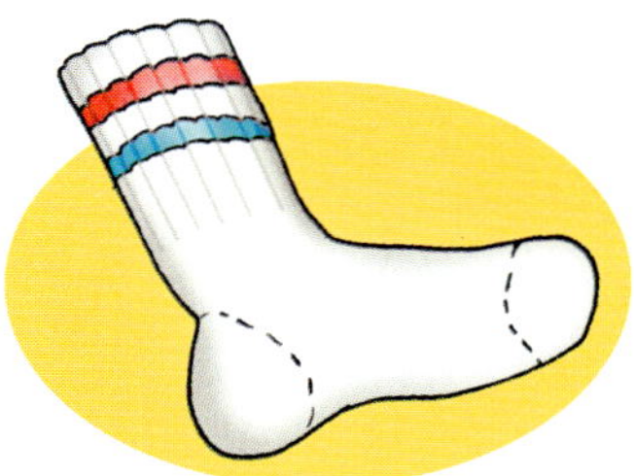

UNIT 6

VOCABULARY & CONCEPT DEVELOPMENT

Common Words in Basic Categories (Identifying, Sorting, Classifying)

Colors
Shapes
Classroom Objects
Toys
Clothing
Food
Living Things (Levels of Specificity):
Plants & Trees, Birds, Insects, Animals, People

Root Words & Inflections

Adjectives with *er, est*

Synonyms

Antonyms

Multiple Meaning Words

Homonyms (Same Sound, Same Spelling)
Homographs (Same Spelling, Different Sounds)

Homophones

(Different Meanings & Spellings, Same Sound)

Simple Prefixes & Suffixes

un–, re–, dis–; –ly, –ful, –less

Compound Words

Multisyllabic Words

Review & Expansion

Multisyllabic Word Game (Classifying & Syllabication)

The number indicates the page on which the word first appears. If a student has difficulty decoding or recognizing a word, refer to that page for more practice.

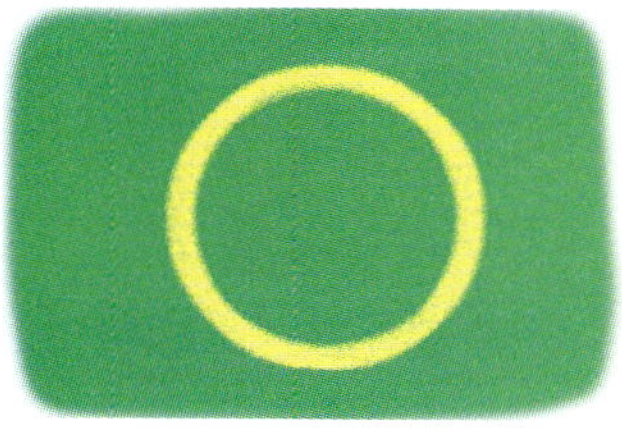

circle

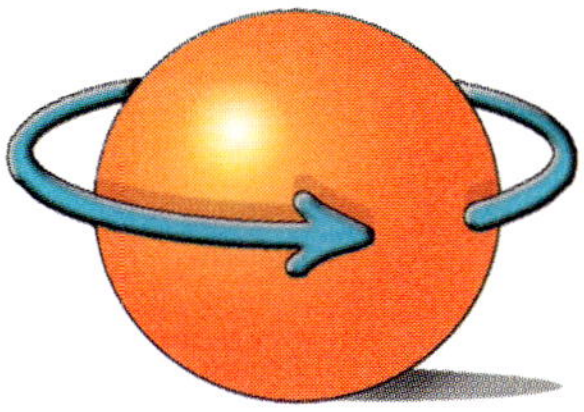

round

triangle

rectangle

square

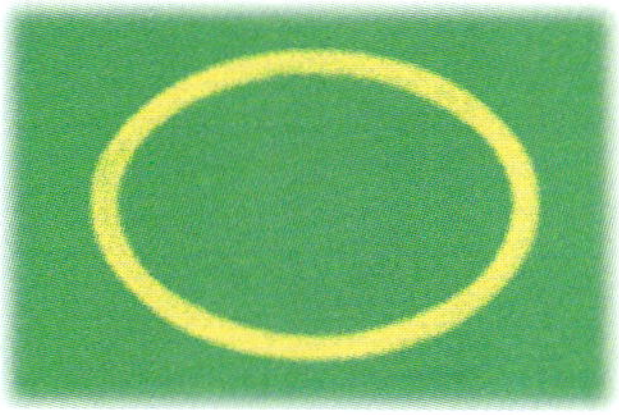

oval

"What do you see?"

"I see a yellow circle, five green triangles, a pink square, and a brown rectangle. And you?"

"I see a girl sitting on a bench in a park on a sunny day."

Classroom Objects

desk
73

globe
114

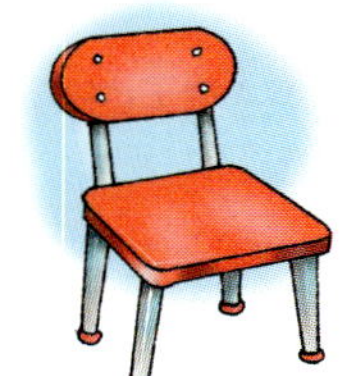

chair
129

book
152

paper
157

crayon
157

pencil
160

chalk
167

Toys

doll
77

yo-yo
124

The number indicates the page on which the word first appears. If a student has difficulty decoding or recognizing a word, refer to that page for more practice.

Clothing

cap
11

hat
24

dress
75

coat
130

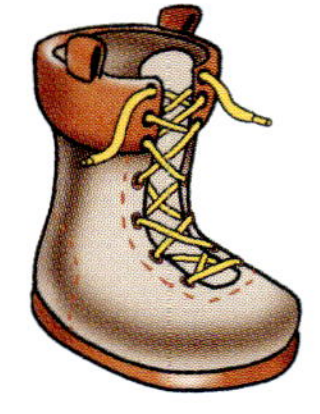

boot
132

shirt
138

skirt
138

sneaker
157

mitten
159

jacket
160

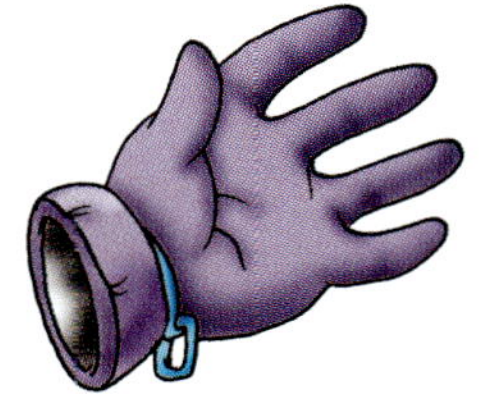

glove
162

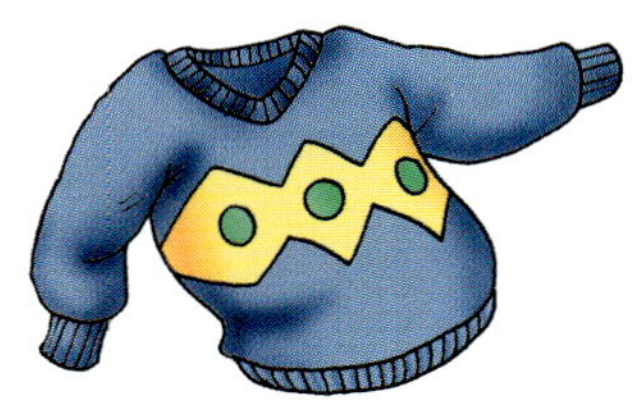

sweater
163

Food

The number indicates the page on which the word first appears. If a student has difficulty decoding or recognizing a word, refer to that page for more practice.

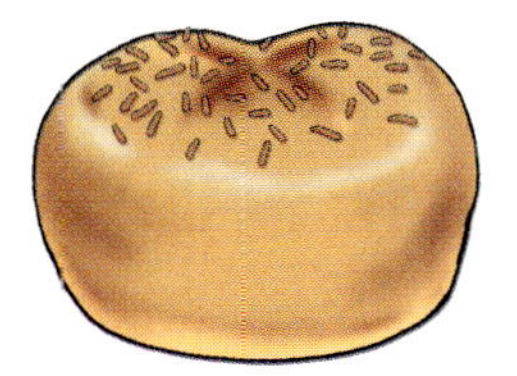

roll
135

corn
139

flour
146

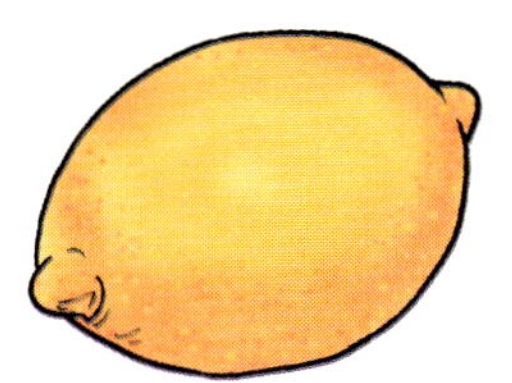

lemon
156

muffin
158

butter
159

honey
162

bread
163

apple
164

noodle
165

cheese
175

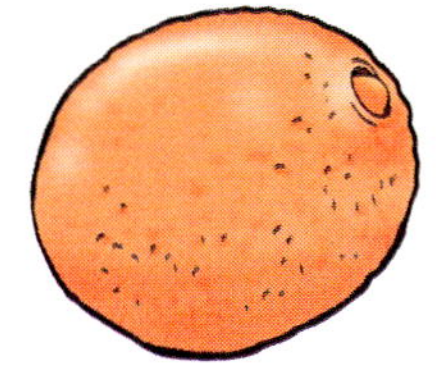

orange
176

Plants & Trees

pine
112

bush
153

flower
156

rose
175

Birds

jay
128

crow
131

owl
147

eagle
165

Insects

ant
37

bee
120

The number indicates the page on which the word first appears. If a student has difficulty decoding or recognizing a word, refer to that page for more practice.

Animals

fox
74

skunk
89

sheep
121

goat
130

cow
147

camel
156

rabbit
158

monkey
162

People

girl
138

boy
148

	tall	taller	tallest
	fast	faster	fastest

	large big	larger bigger g → gg	largest biggest g → gg
  	hot	hotter t → tt	hottest t → tt

	happy	happier y → i	happiest y → i
  	heavy	heavier y → i	heaviest y → i

close
shut

ship
boat

shop
store

mad
angry

big
large

little
small

gift
present

bunny
rabbit

shout
yell

over
above

song
tune

sad
unhappy

hot

cold

big

little

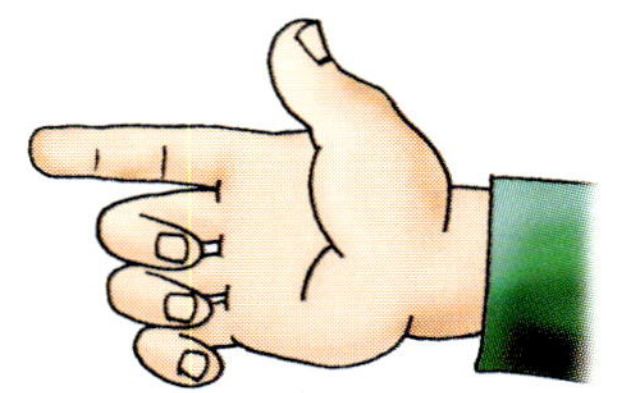

left

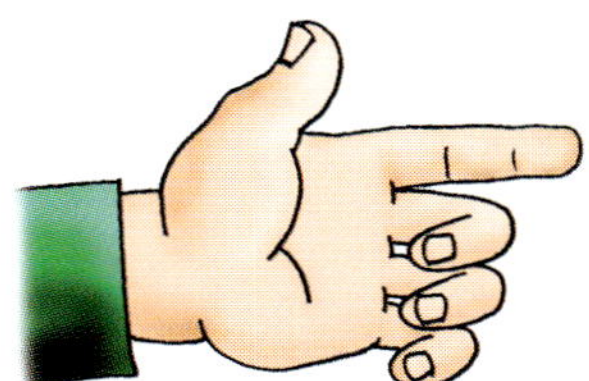

right

happy

sad

day

night

last

first

 new

 old

 up

 down

 over

 under

 tall

 short

 pull

 push

 close

 open

Homonyms (Same Sound, Same Spelling)

fall

ring

bat

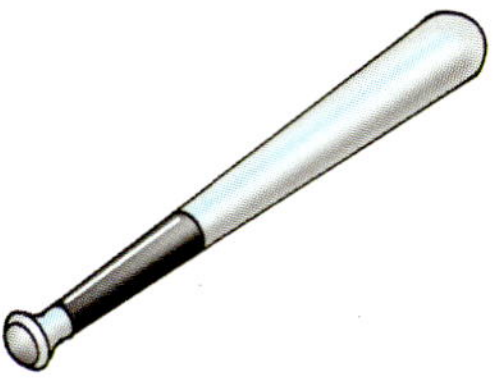

fly

orange

mouse

top

saw

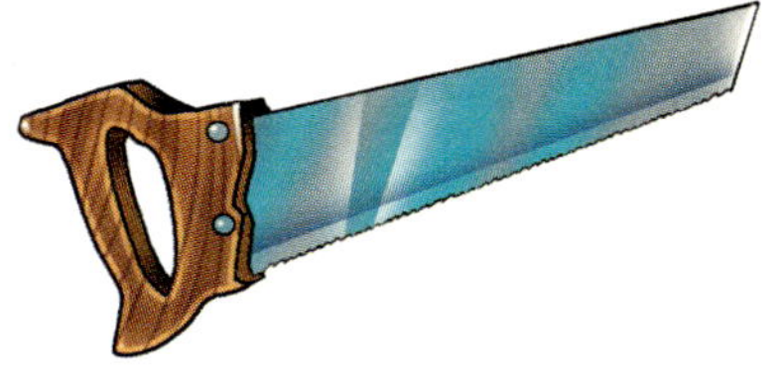

cut

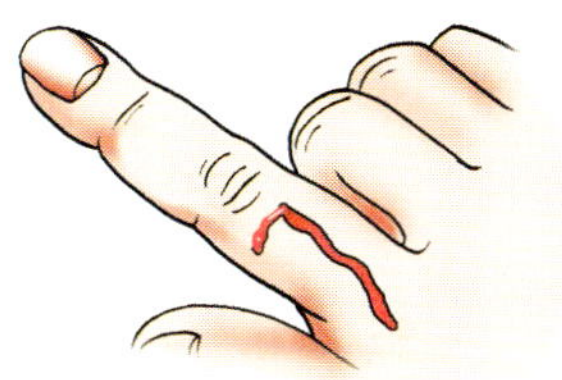

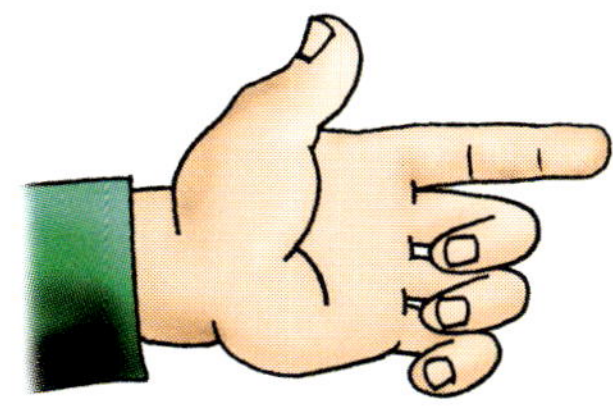

right

Homographs (Same Spelling, Different Sounds)

bow

bow

wind

wind

sea

see

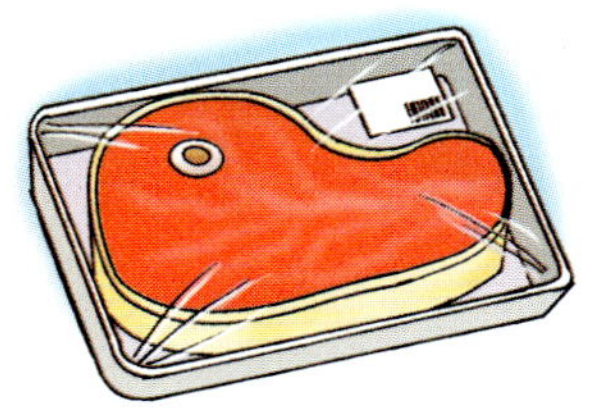

meat

meet

ate

eight

write

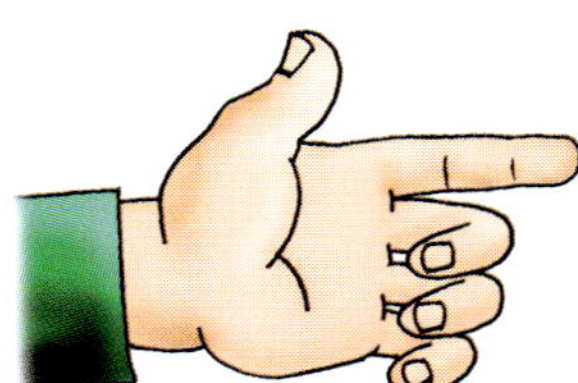

right

rap

wrap

flour

flower

un-		unhappy		unfold
re-		rewrite		return
dis-		disconnect		disappear
-ly		slowly		quickly
-ful		careful		playful
-less		homeless		weightless

bedroom

classroom

lunchroom

lunchbox

mailbox

sandbox

notebook

bookshelf

backpack

backyard

raincoat

rainbow

snowman

snowball

football

basketball

sunrise

sunset

armchair

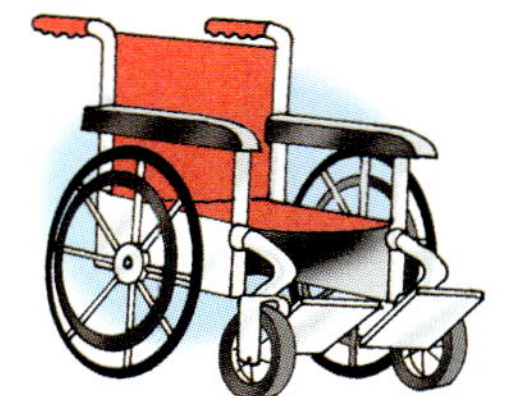

wheelchair

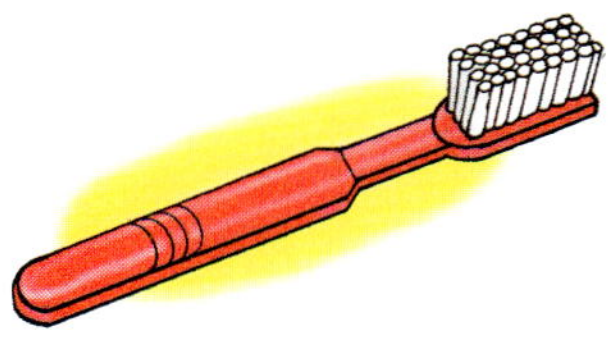

toothbrush

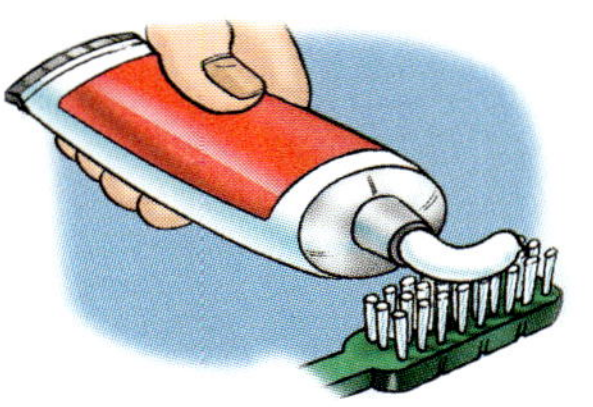

toothpaste

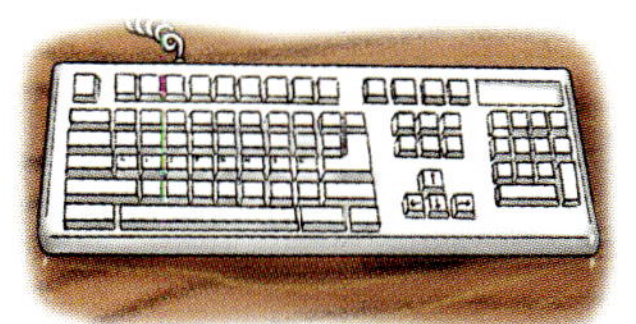

keyboard

skateboard

alligator

butterfly

caterpillar

dragonfly

elevator

flamingo

grasshopper

hippopotamus

invitation

jellyfish

kangaroo

ladybug

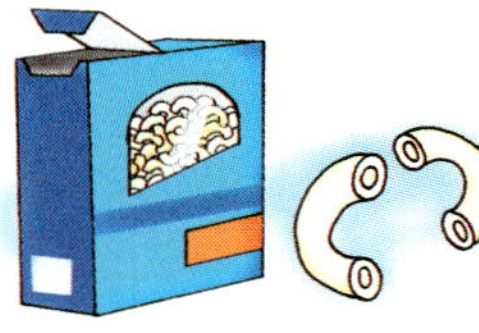
macaroni

newspaper

octopus

porcupine

quarter

refrigerator

strawberry

telescope

umbrella

videotape

woodpecker

xylophone

yogurt

zebra

"I'm thinking of an insect that starts with the letter *g* and has three syllables."

"Is it a grasshopper?"

"Yes! That's right!"

I'm thinking of ______________________
an insect / an animal / a bird / a food / an object

that starts with the letter ____ and has

____ syllables.

Students use the words on pages 198–199 to play this word game. The game can also be played with all the categories and words on pages 180–187.

above

act
actor

add

alligator

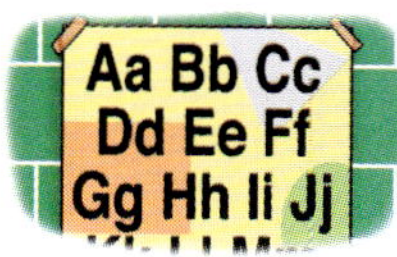

alphabet

angry

ant

apple

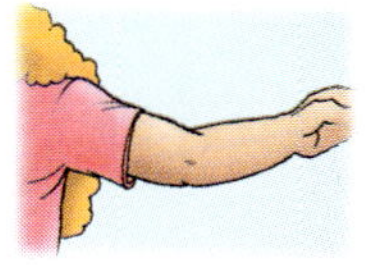
arm

armchair

ask

baby

back

backpack

backyard

bad

bag

bake
baker

ball

band

bang

bank

bark

barn

basketball

bat

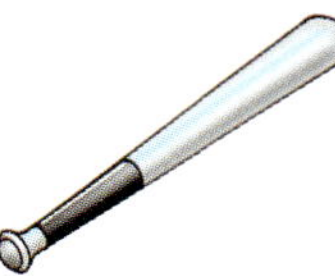
bat

bath

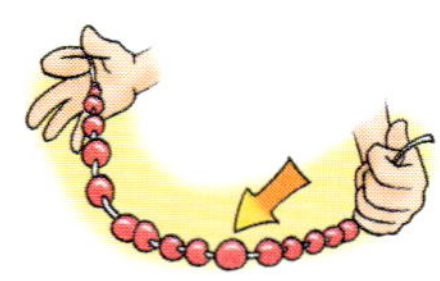
bead

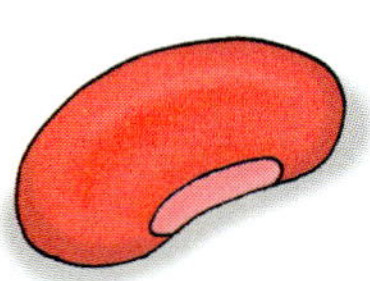
bean

beat

bed

bedroom

bee

beetle

beg

bell

belt

bench

bend – bent

best

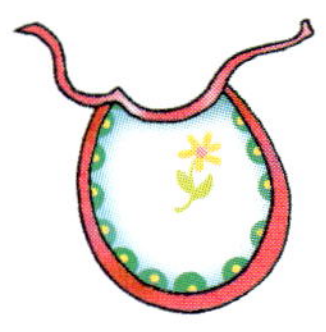
bib

big

bike

bird

bite – bit

black

blank

blanket

blind

blink

block

blow – blew

blue

boat

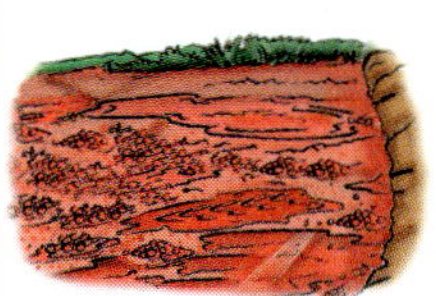
bog

boil

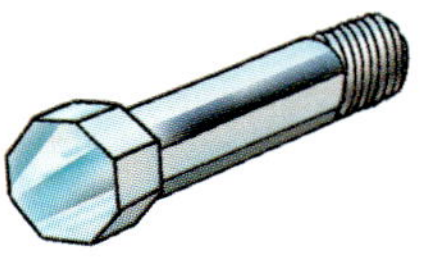
bolt

bone

book

bookshelf

boot

bottom

bow

bow

box

boy

brace

branch

bread

breakfast

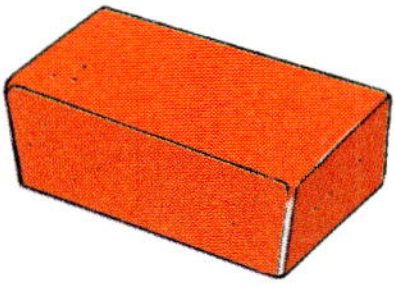
brick

bright

bring–
brought

broke

broken

brook

broom

brother

brown

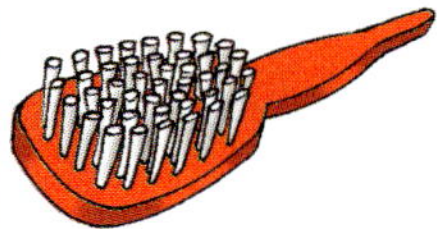
brush

bubble

bud

bug

bull

bump

bun

bunk

 bunny

 bus

 bush

 busy

 butter

 butterfly

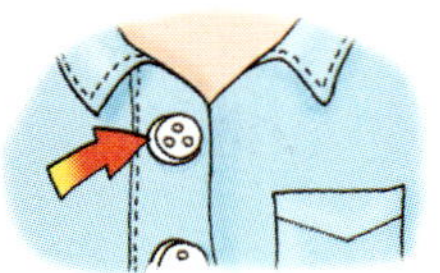 button

 cabin

 cake

 calf–calves

 call

 camel

 camp

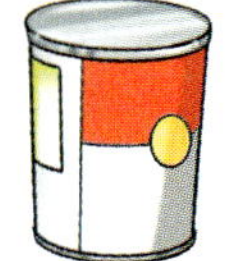 can

 cane

 cap

 cape

 car

 card

 careful

 cart

 castle

 cat

 catch–caught

 caterpillar

 chain

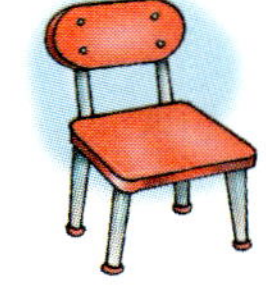 chair

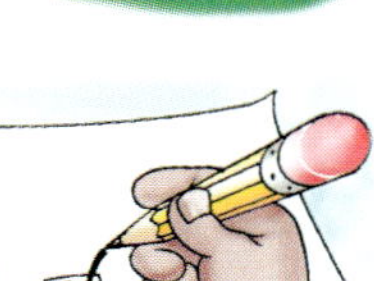

chalk

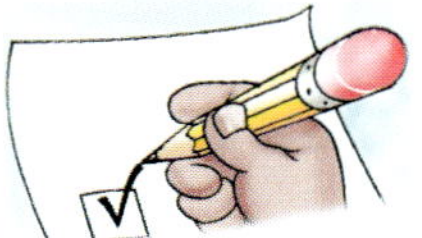 check

cheese

chess

chest

chick

chicken

child–
children

chimp

chin

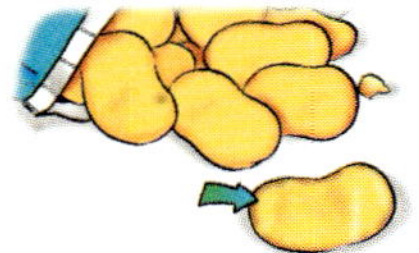
chip

choose

chop

church

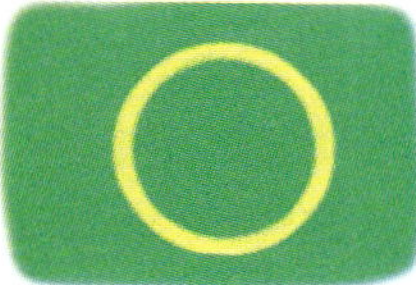
circle

clam

clap

class
classroom

clay

clean

cliff

climb

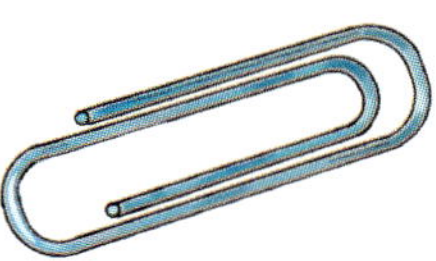
clip

clock

close

cloud

clown

club

coat

cod

coin

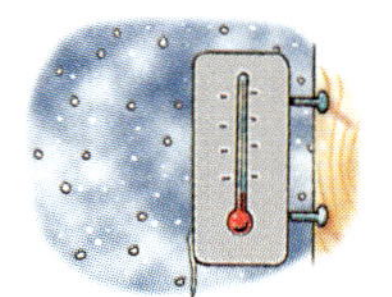
cold

colt

comb

come

conduct
conductor

cone

cook

corn

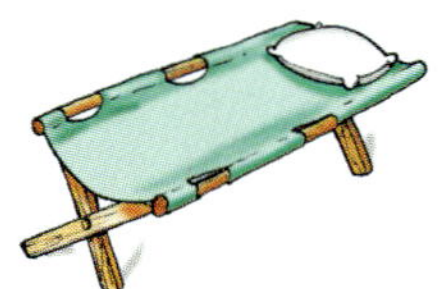
cot

cough

count

cow

crab

cradle

crank

crash

crayon

crop

crow

crust

cry

cub

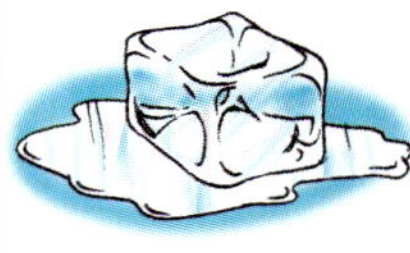
cube

cup

curl

cut

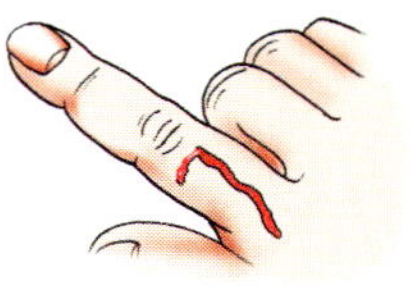
cut

cute

dad

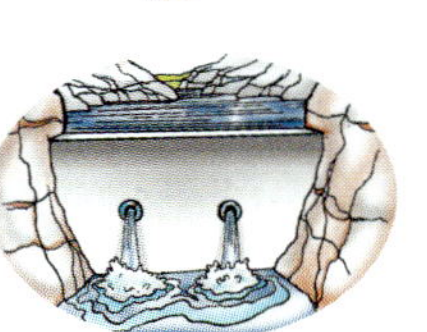
dam

dance
dancer

dark

day

deer

den

dent

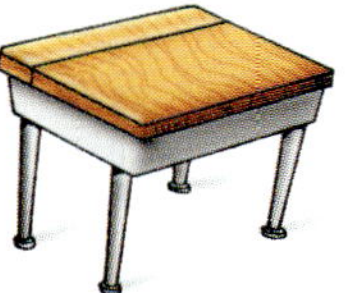
desk

dig–dug

dime

ding dong

dinner

dip

dirty

disappear

disconnect

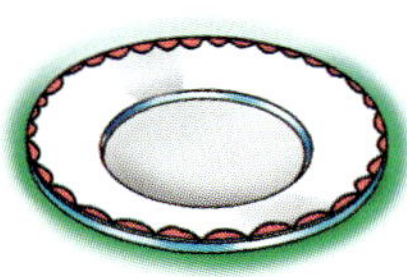
dish

disk

ditch

dive

doctor

dog

doll

dollar

dolphin

dome

donkey

door

dot

down

dragon

dragonfly

draw

dream

dress

drink–
drank

drive–
drove

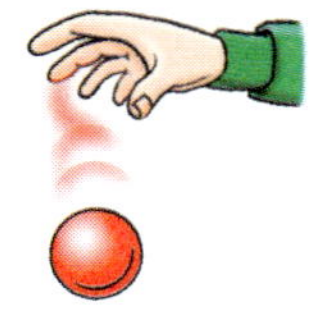
drop

drum

dry

duck

duke

dump

dune

dust

Dutch

E

eagle

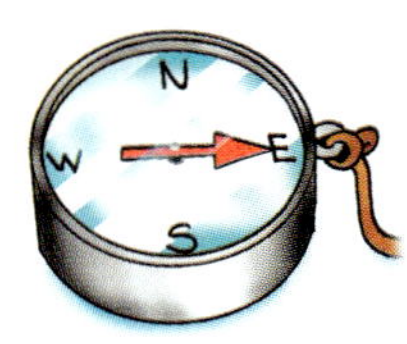

east

easy

eat–
ate

egg

elephant

elevator

elf–
elves

elk

F

face

fall–
fell

fall

fan

fang

far

farm
farmer

fast

fat

father

feather

feed–
fed

fern

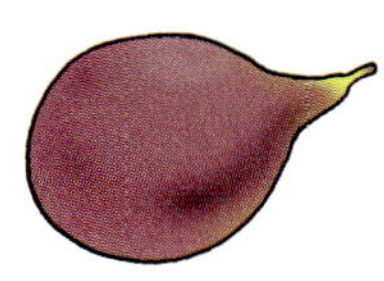
fig

fill

fin

find

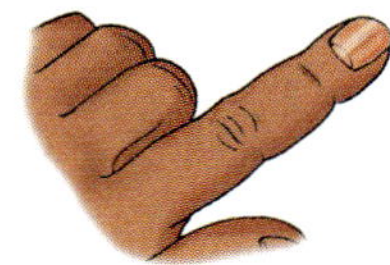
finger

first

fish

fist

fit

fix

flag

flamingo

flap

flat

flip

float

floor

flour

flower

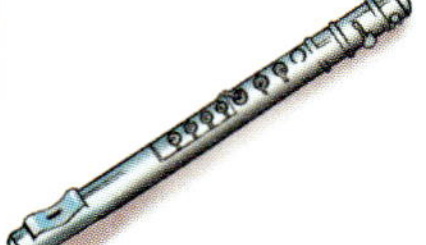
flute

fly

fly –
flew

fog

foil

fold

follow

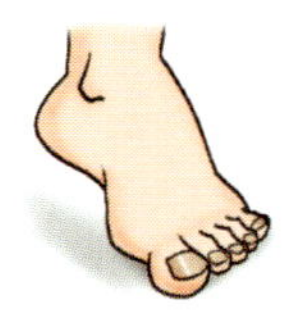
foot –
feet

football

fork

fox

frog

fry

full

fun

game

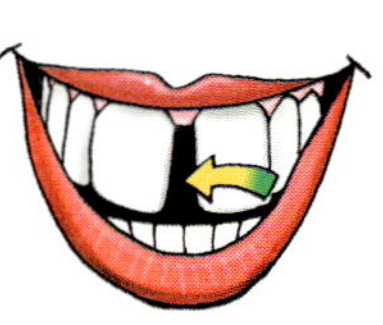
gap

gas

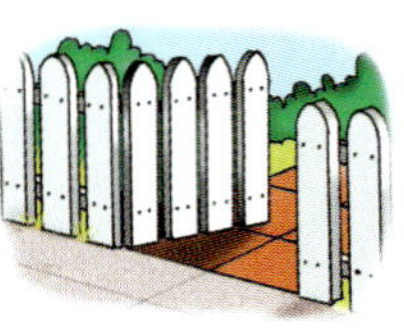
gate

get –
got

giant

gift

gill

giraffe

girl

give –
gave

glass

globe

glove

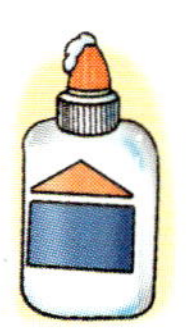
glue

go—went

goat

gold

good

goose—geese

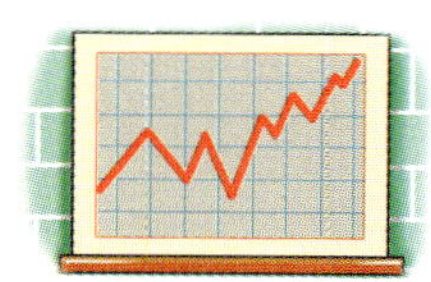
graph

grass

grasshopper

gray

green

grow—grew

gull

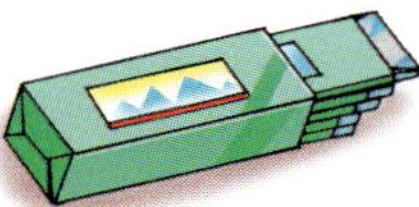
gum

H

half

hall

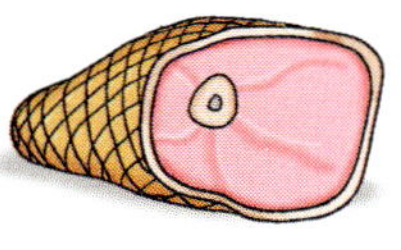
ham

hammer

hand

hang

happy

harp

has

hat

have

hay

he

head

heavy

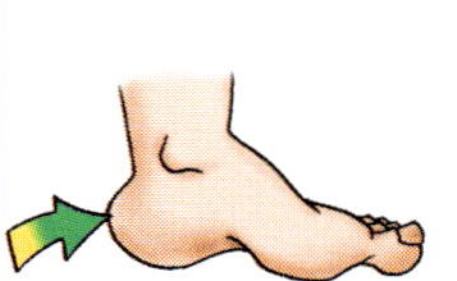
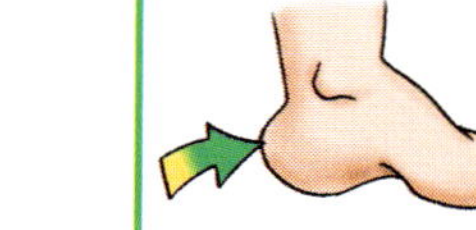
heel

hen

herd

hide

high

hike

hill

hip

hippopotamus

hit

hive

hoe

hog

hold

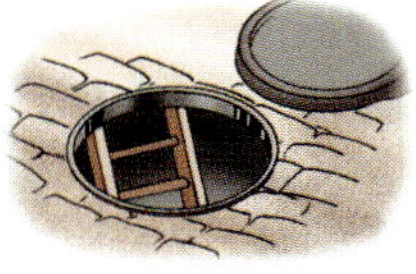
hole

home

homeless

honey

hook

hop

horn

hose

hot

house

how

huff

hug

hump

hunt

hurt

hut

ice

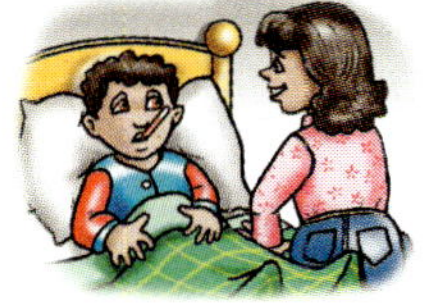
ill

inch

insect

invitation

itch

jacket

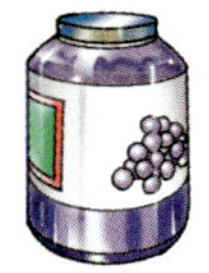
jam

jar

jay

jeep

jellyfish

jet

jig

job

jog
jogger

jug

jump

junk

kangaroo

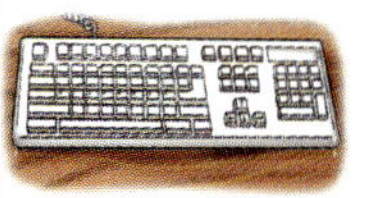
keyboard

kick

kid

kind

king

King Kong

kiss

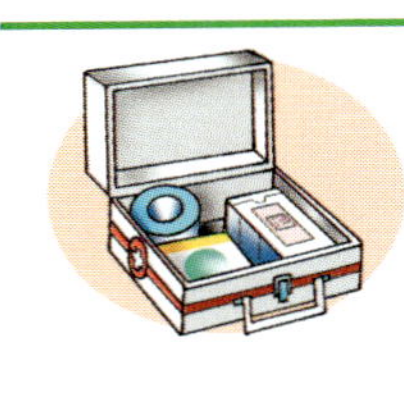 kit

 kite

 kitten

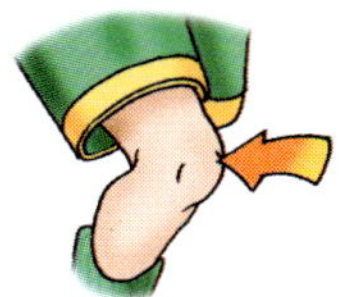 knee

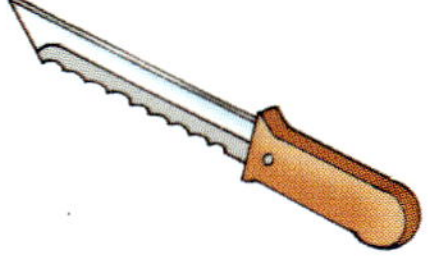 knife–knives

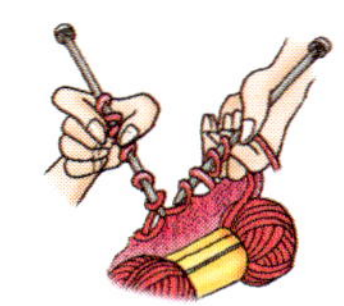 knit

 knock

 lad

 ladder

 ladybug

 lamb

 lamp

 lane

 lap

 large

 last

 laugh

 leaf–leaves

 led

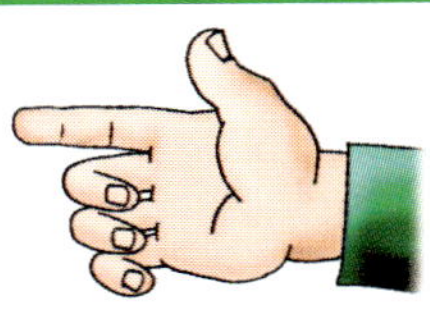 left

 leg

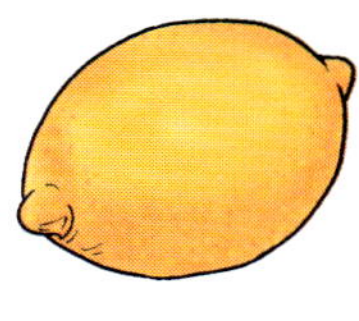 lemon

letter

 lift

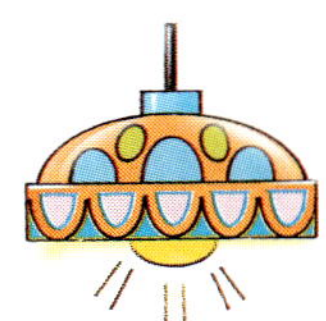 light

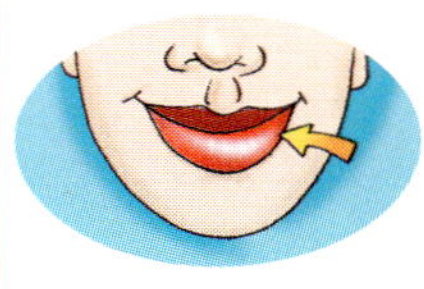 lip

list

 listen

 lit

little

loaf – loaves

lock

log

long

look

lot

low

luck

lunch

lunchbox

lunchroom

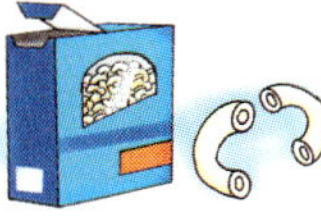
macaroni

mad

mailbox

man – men

mane

map

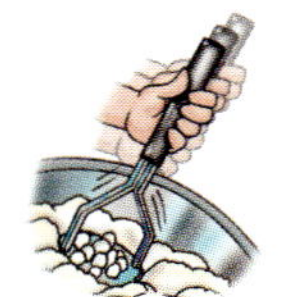
mash

mask

mat

math

me

meal

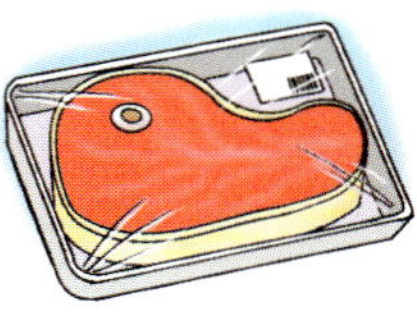
meat

meet – met

melt

mend

middle

milk

mill

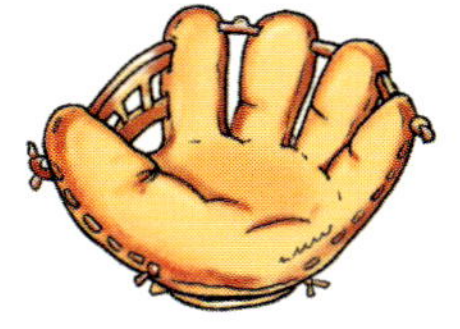
mitt

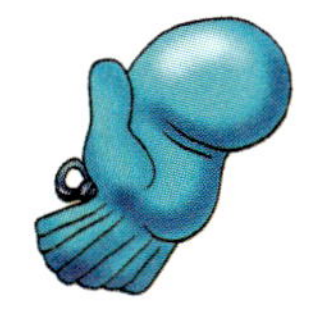
mitten

mix

mole

mom

money

monkey

moon

mop

mother

mouse – mice

mouse

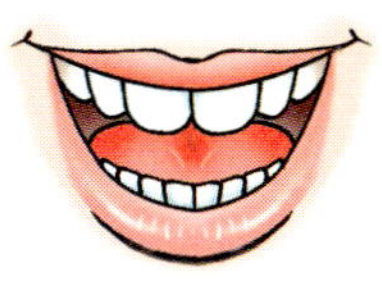
mouth

mud

muffin

mug

mule

my

name

nap

neck

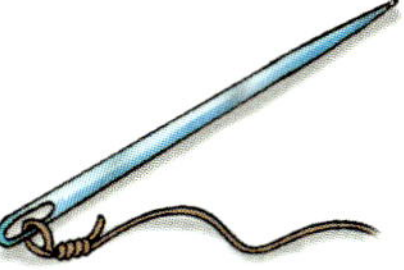
needle

nest

net

new

newspaper

night

nit

no

nod

none

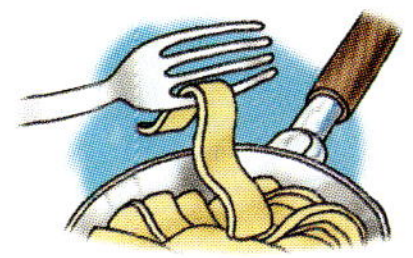
noodle

north

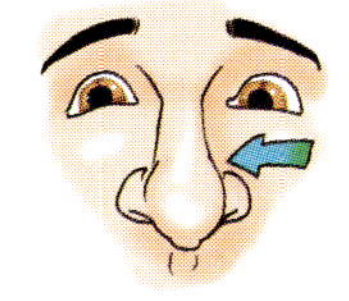
nose

not

note

notebook

nut

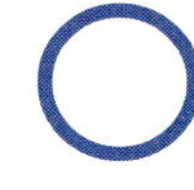
O

oar

octopus

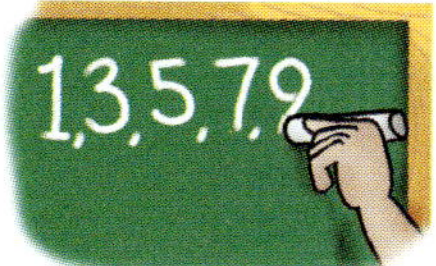

odd

off

oil

old

on

open

orange

orange

our

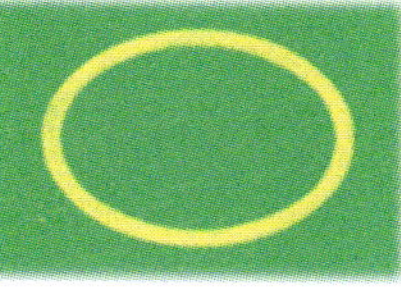
oval

over

owl

P

pad

pail

paint
painter

pan

paper

park

patch

path

pea

peach

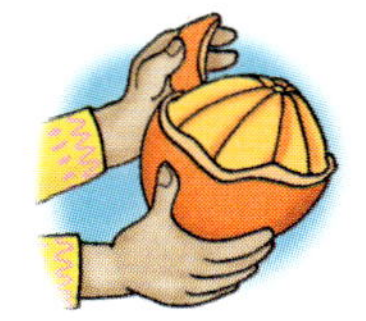
peel

pen

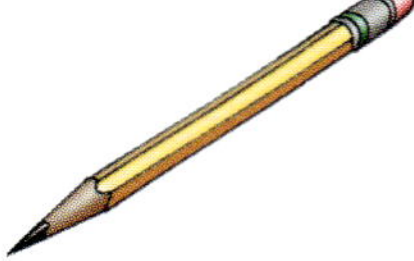
pencil

penny—pennies

pet

phone

photo

pick

pig

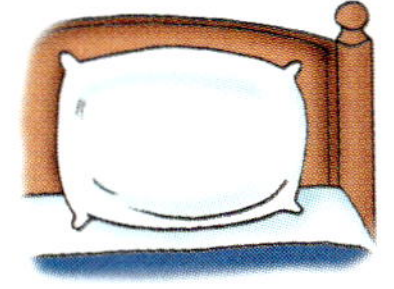
pillow

pin

pinch

pine

ping pong

pink

pipe

pit

pitch

plane

planet

plant

plate

play

playful

please

point

pole

pond

pony

poodle

pool

pop

porcupine

pot

pour

present

press

princess

print

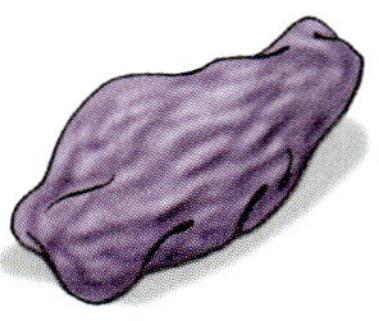
prune

puddle

puff

pull

pup

puppet

puppy–
puppies

purple

push

put

puzzle

quack

quarter

queen

quick
quickly

quill

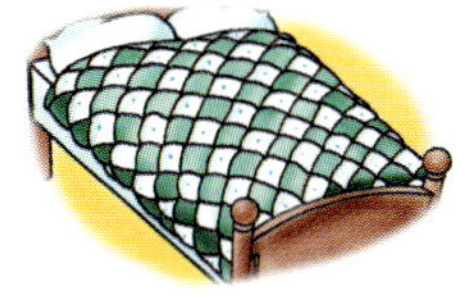
quilt

quit

quiz

R

rabbit

race

raft

rag

rain

rainbow

raincoat

rake

ramp

ranch

rap

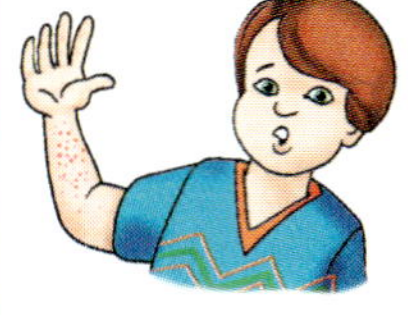
rash

rat

read

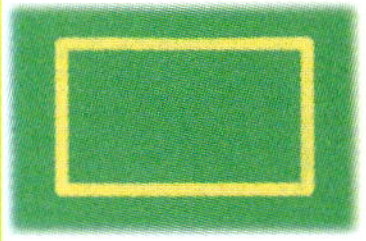
rectangle

red

refrigerator

rest

return

rewrite

rice

rich

ride–
rode

rig

right

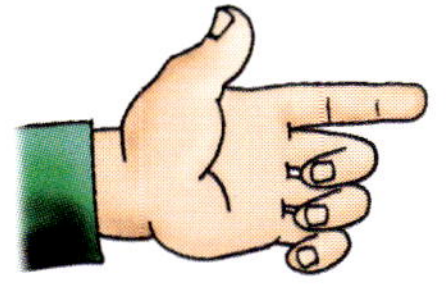
right

ring–
rang

ring

rink

rip

road

roar

robe

rock

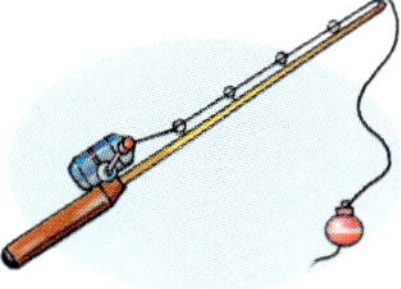
rod

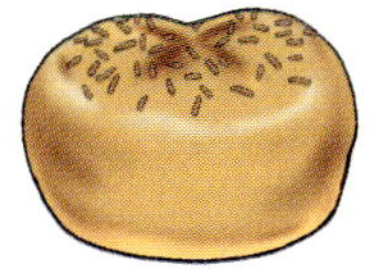
roll

rose

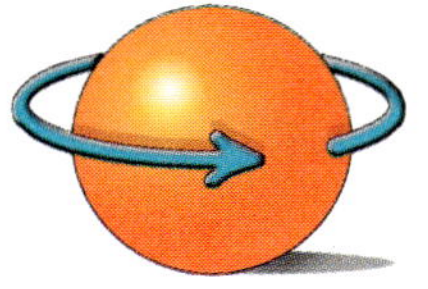
round

row

rub

rude

rug

rule

ruler

run–
ran

rut

S

sack

sad

sail

sand

sandbox

sap

sauce

save

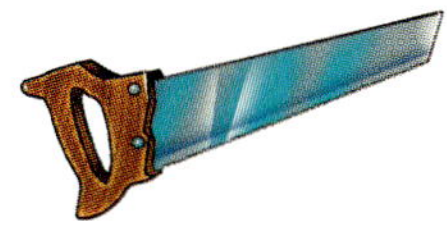
saw

say – said

score

scratch

scream

sea

seal

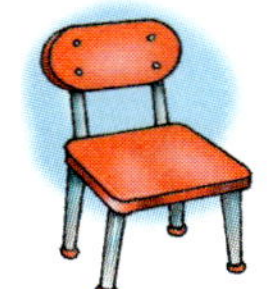
seat

see – saw

seed

sell – sold

set

shadow

shark

sharp

she

shed

sheep

shelf – shelves

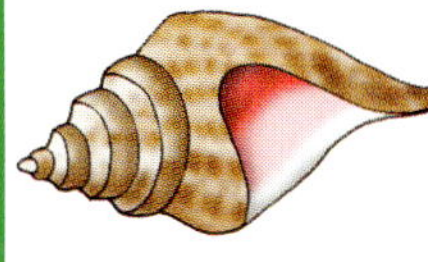
shell

ship

shirt

shop

shop shopper

short

shout

shovel

shut

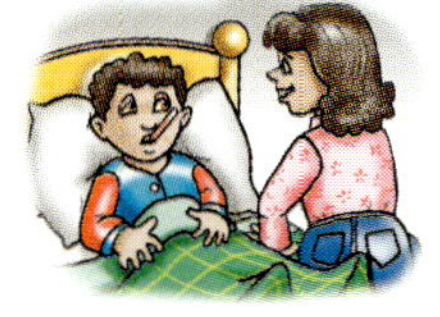
sick

side

sigh

sing–
sang

singer

sink

sip

sister

sit–
sat

skate

skateboard

sketch

skin

skip

skirt

skunk

sky

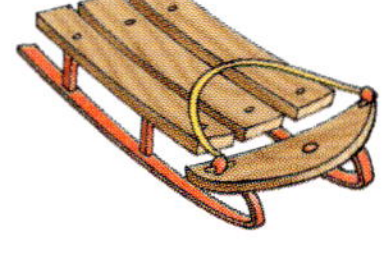
sled

sleep

sleepy

sleigh

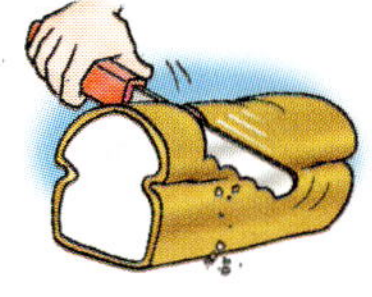
slice

slide

sling

slip

slot

slowly

slug

small

smart

smell

smog

smoke

snake

sneaker

snow

snowball

snowman

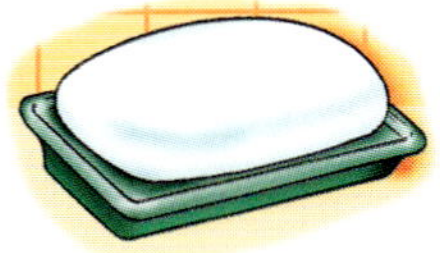
soap

sob

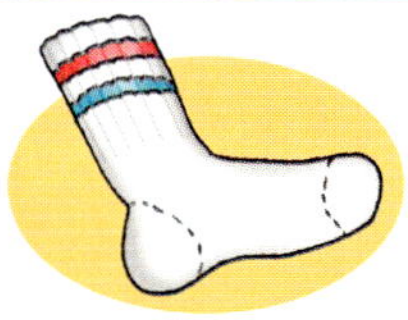
sock

soil

some

song

soup

south

space

spell

spider

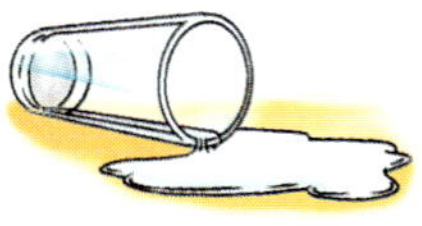
spill

spin

splash

split

spoon

spot

spray

spring

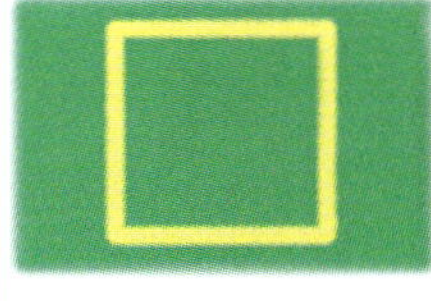
square

squirrel

stamp

stand

star

steeple

stem

step

stick

sting

stink

stir

stole

stool

stop

store

storm

stove

straw

strawberry

street

stretch

string

study

sub

summer

sun

sunrise

sunset

supper

swap

sweater

sweep

swim
swimmer

swing

switch

table

tag

tail

talk

tall

tan

tank

tap

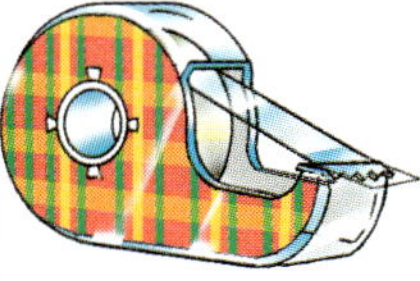
tape

teach –
taught

teacher

team

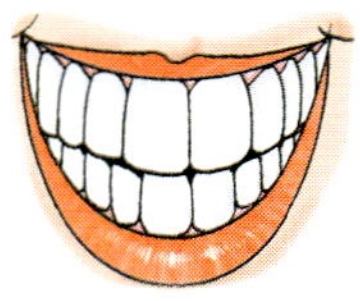
teeth

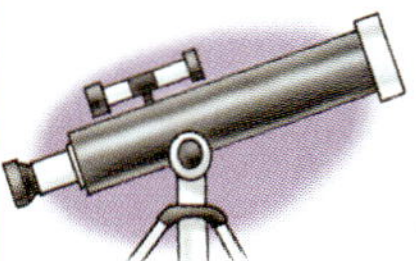
telescope

tell –
told

tent

test

thank

that

these

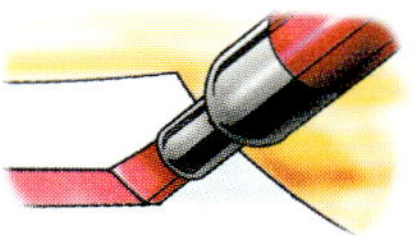
thick

thin

thing

think –
thought

this

those

thread

throw—
threw

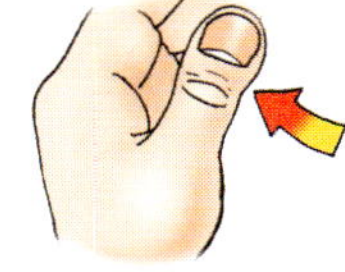
thumb

tick

tickle

time

tiny

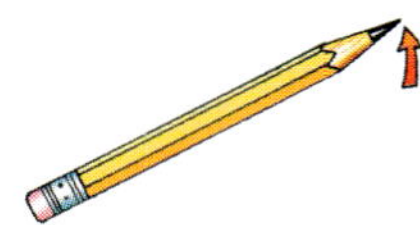
tip

toad

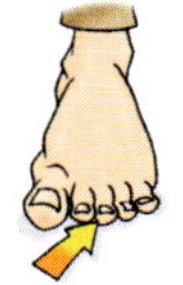
toe

toll

took

tooth

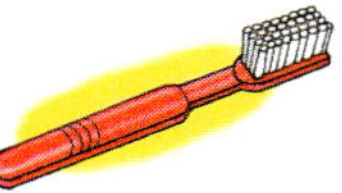
toothbrush

toothpaste

top

top

tot

town

toy

track

tractor

train

trap

trash

tree

triangle

trick

trot

truck

trunk

tub

tube

tug

tune

turn

turtle

umbrella

under

unfold

unhappy

up

us

van

vat

vest

vet

videotape

vote

wag

wagon

walk

wall

was

watch

wax

we

weather

weigh

weight

weightless

well

went

were

west

wet

whale

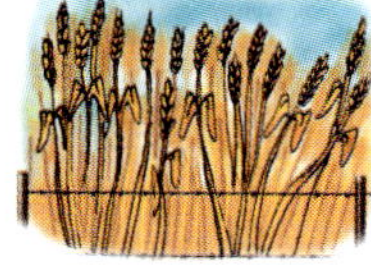
wheat

wheel

wheelchair

when

which

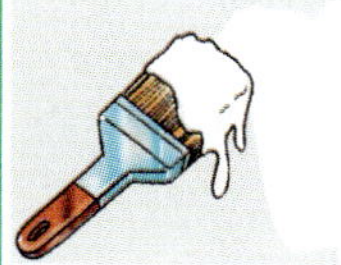
white

why

wig

wild

win
winner

wind
windy

wind

window

wing

wink

winter

wipe

wish

with

wolf–
wolves

woman—women

wood

woodpecker

wool

work

wrap

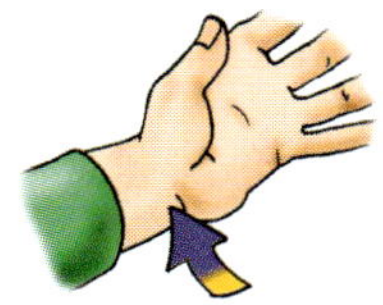
wrist

write

wrong

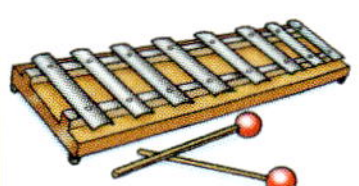
xylophone

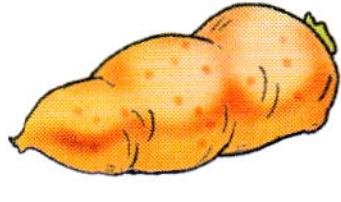
yam

yard

yarn

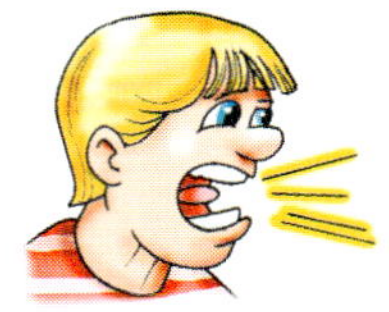
yell

yellow

yo-yo

yogurt

you

Z

zebra

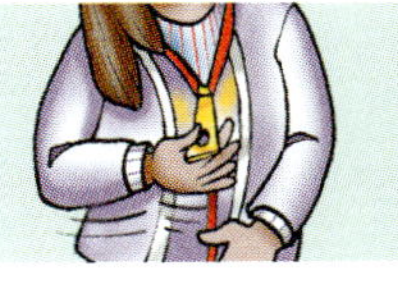
zip

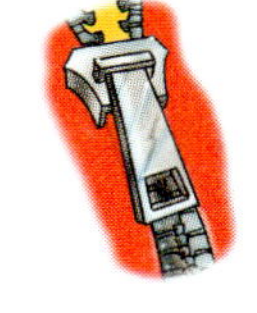
zipper

zit

zoo

NUMBERS

1	one	11	eleven	20	twenty
2	two	12	twelve	30	thirty
3	three	13	thirteen	40	forty
4	four	14	fourteen	50	fifty
5	five	15	fifteen	60	sixty
6	six	16	sixteen	70	seventy
7	seven	17	seventeen	80	eighty
8	eight	18	eighteen	90	ninety
9	nine	19	nineteen	100	one hundred
10	ten				

DAYS

SUN	Sun.	Sunday
MON	Mon.	Monday
TUE	Tues.	Tuesday
WED	Wed.	Wednesday
THU	Thurs.	Thursday
FRI	Fri.	Friday
SAT	Sat.	Saturday

PLACES & ABBREVIATIONS

Ave.	Avenue
Blvd.	Boulevard
Fwy.	Freeway
Hwy.	Highway
Pl.	Place
Rd.	Road
St.	Street
Tpk.	Turnpike
N.	North
S.	South
E.	East
W.	West

MONTHS

JAN	Jan.	January
FEB	Feb.	February
MAR	Mar.	March
APR	Apr.	April
MAY	May	May
JUN	June	June
JUL	July	July
AUG	Aug.	August
SEP	Sept.	September
OCT	Oct.	October
NOV	Nov.	November
DEC	Dec.	December

TITLES & ABBREVIATIONS

For a man:

Mr.

For a woman:

Miss

Ms.

Mrs.

Numbers indicate the pages on which words appear. (Review lessons are not included in this listing.)

above **162, 189**
act **174**
actor **174**
add **37, 172**
added **172**
adding **172**
adds **172**
alligator **198**
alphabet **176**
angry **161, 189**
ant **37, 70, 186**
apple **164, 185**
arm **137**
armchair **197**
ask **73**
ate **111, 194**

babies **169**
baby **126, 169**
back **78**
backpack **196**
backyard **196**
bad **25**
bag **26, 46**
bake **110, 173, 174**
baked **173**
baker **157, 174**
bakes **173**
baking **173**
ball **150**
band **69**
bang **86**
bank **88**
bark **136**
barn **137**
basketball **197**
bat **10, 24, 46, 192**
bath **85**
bead **122**
bean **122, 184**
beat **123**
bed **46**
bedroom **196**
bee **120, 186**
beetle **165**
beg **46**
bell **76**
belt **71**
Ben **33**
bench **90**
bend **69**
bent **70**
best **72**
Beth **85**
bib **46**
big **12, 27, 46, 188, 189, 190**
bigger **188**
biggest **188**
bike **112, 168**
bikes **168**
bird **138**
bit **29, 118**
bite **113, 118**
black **78, 180**
blank **88**
blanket **160**
blew **133**
blind **135**
blink **88**
block **79**
blow **131**
blue **133, 180**
boat **130, 189**
Bob **46**
bog **31, 46**
boil **148**
bolt **135**
bone **115**
book **152, 168, 182**
books **168**
bookshelf **196**
boot **132, 183**
bottom **6**
bow **131, 147, 193**
box **74, 168**
boxes **168**
boy **148, 187**
brace **125**
branch **90**
bread **163, 185**
breakfast **163**
brick **78**
bright **154**
bring **86**
broke **114**
broken **157**
brook **152**
broom **132**
brother **162**
brought **154**
brown **147, 180**
brush **84, 168, 172**
brushed **172**
brushes **168, 172**
brushing **172**
bubble **164**
bud **36**
bug **21, 34, 46**
bull **153**
bump **68**
bun **20, 35**
bunk **89**
bunny **126, 189**
bus **46**
bush **153, 186**
busy **175**
butter **159, 185**
butterfly **198**
button **159**

cabin **156**
cake **110, 184**
calf **167, 169**
call **150**
calves **169**
camel **156, 187**
camp **68**
can **9, 22, 51, 119**
cane **110, 119**
cap **11, 23, 119, 183**
cape **111, 119**
car **136**
card **136**
careful **195**
cart **137**
castle **167**
cat **10, 24, 51**
catch **91**
caterpillar **198**
caught **155**
chain **129**
chair **129, 182**
chalk **167, 182**
check **82**
cheese **175, 185**
chess **82**
chest **82**
chick **82**
chicken **160**
child **134, 170**
children **170**
chimp **82**
chin **82**
chip **82**
choose **175**
chop **82**
church **138**
circle **164, 181**
clam **64**
clap **64**
class **75**
classroom **196**
clay **128**
clean **122, 172**
cleaned **172**
cleaning **172**
cleans **172**
cliff **75**
climb **167**
clip **64**
clock **79**
close **175, 189, 191**
cloud **146**
clown **147**
club **64**
coat **130, 183**
cod **51**
coin **148**
cold **134, 190**
colt **135**
comb **167**
come **177**
conduct **174**
conductor **174**
cone **115**
cook **152, 172**
cooked **172**
cooking **172**
cooks **172**
corn **139, 185**
cot **17, 30, 51**
cough **176**
count **146**
cow **147, 187**
crab **65**
cradle **165**
crank **88**
crash **84**
crayon **157, 182**
crop **65**
crow **131, 186**
crust **73**
cry **127**
cub **36, 51, 119**
cube **116, 119**
cup **36**
curl **138**
cut **35, 51, 119, 193**
cute **117, 119**

dad **25, 48**
dam **26, 48**
dance **174**
dancer **174**
dark **136**
day **128, 190**
deer **170**
den **33, 48**
dent **70**
desk **73, 182**
dig **27, 48**
dime **112**
ding dong **87**
dinner **158**
dip **14, 28, 48**
dirty **161**
disappear **195**
disconnect **195**
dish **84**
disk **73**
ditch **91**
dive **113**
doctor **160**
dog **149**
doll **48, 77, 182**
dollar **158**
dolphin **176**
dome **115**
donkey **162**
door **151**
dot **30, 48**
down **147, 191**
dragon **156**
dragonfly **198**
drank **88**
draw **149**
dream **122**
dress **75, 183**
drew **133**
drink **88**
drive **113**